WITHDRAWN

D1126500

MIDDLINGNESS

Juste Milieu
Political Theory in
France and England, 1815–48

MIDDLINGNESS

Juste Milieu
Political Theory in
France and England, 1815–48

Vincent E. Starzinger
Dartmouth College

The University Press of Virginia
Charlottesville

CALVIN T. RYAN LIBRARY
KEARNEY STATE COLLEGE
KEARNEY, NEBRASKA

Copyright © 1965
by the Rector and Visitors
of the University of Virginia

THE UNIVERSITY PRESS OF VIRGINIA

First published 1965

Library of Congress
Catalog Card Number: 65–23999
Printed in the
United States of America

93397

320. 5
St28

Dedicated to

"Sir Claude Mulhammer"
of T. S. Eliot's
The Confidential Clerk

AMONG other recurring attitudes in politics, apparently there exists what can be called, almost in an a priori sense, the "middling mind." In any political context, whether the extremes of left and right are formidable or negligible, there are invariably those who crave the middle way. France since the Revolution, for example, has more than once been rent by seemingly irreconcilable extremes, but has never lacked at least a handful of faithful middling souls who sought to construct a viable center out of thin air. Or, to take quite a different context, witness the persistence of the Liberals in Britain as a middle party between a Tory party and a Labour party which over the years have moved closer together ideologically, rather than farther apart. Again, although one hesitates to comment on contemporary America, perhaps a passing word is not inappropriate. For if "moderation" surely seems a worthy and relevant cause in American politics at the precise date of this writing, one can also remember that only a few years back the American fetish for casting issues in terms of the "middle of the road" sometimes seemed something of a puzzle. By that I mean that the ideological extremes then seemed so negligible that the preoccupation with avoiding them often struck one as irrelevant. Of course from hindsight one may be tempted to argue that the present state of our politics simply proves the wisdom of those who all along have warned against any explorations to the left or right of dead center. However, one can also argue to the contrary that an important cause of extremist politics in the

1960s may have been the willingness of most Americans during the 1950s to accept a vacuous policy, one which could almost be called moderation purely for the sake of moderation, as a substitute for the imaginative, effective solution of issues which were becoming more serious with each passing year.

In any event, the ubiquity of the middling mind surely seems provocative in terms of the study of political theory. Yet, for all the studies of revolution and reaction in modern Western political development, there has been surprisingly little depth analysis of middlingness. Its friends naturally assure us, as did Halifax, "true virtue hath ever been thought a trimmer, and to have its dwelling place midway between the two extremes."[1] On the other hand, the enemies of middlingness are forever describing it as either the way of shallow opportunism or as a good place to be crushed from both sides. Although any one of these observations may on occasion be accurate, they do not do justice to the full range of strategic, intellectual, and psychological implications and problems of the center position in politics.

The two particular contexts in which this essay studies those implications and problems are the attempts in France and England after the Napoleonic wars to establish middle-class rule as a permanent *juste milieu* or golden mean between the extremes of revolution and reaction. At the outset I should disclaim any intent to present a comprehensive narrative account of political events in these two countries. Rather, my purpose is to analyze the theory of *juste milieu* as it was developed by four thinkers of the period and, at the same time, project that theory against the broad background of politics and society. In France, I will deal with the ideas of Pierre Paul Royer-Collard and François Pierre Guillaume Guizot. As leaders of that small band of liberals known as

[1] "The Character of a Trimmer," in Walter Raleigh, ed., *The Complete Works of George Savile, First Marquess of Halifax* (Oxford: Clarendon Press, 1912), p. 103.

Doctrinaires,[2] these two were unquestionably the outstanding theorists of the middle-class *juste milieu* which France's July Revolution of 1830 established. Guizot was also a distinguished historian and master of the French cabinet from 1840 to 1848. My choice of those two Reform Whigs, Henry Peter Brougham and Thomas Babington Macaulay, is perhaps not so obvious. For in English *juste milieu* theory no two Whigs held quite the preeminent position of Royer-Collard and Guizot. And in the sense of having come originally from outside that "privileged enclosure" of grandees so often identified as "Whiggery," both Macaulay and Brougham were somewhat atypical.[3] Nevertheless, both were, in 1832, superlatively "men of '32"—highly popular, articulate Parliamentary advocates of the Great Reform Bill with which the Whigs enfranchised the English middle class. In addition to Macaulay's historical works, these two also left rather more extensive political writings than their contemporary Whigs. Finally, and I have no desire to be mysterious, still another explanation for my choice of Brougham and Macaulay will emerge with the conclusion of my analysis, and is perhaps better reserved until then.

Like the problem of middlingness itself, these four theorists have generally received rather brusque treatment at the hands of the commentators. When they are remembered, they are usually placed unsurely on the margin of either left or right,[4] with the result that their preoccupation with mid-

---

[2] As critics always note, "Doctrinaire" was something of a misnomer—given them in 1816 not for inflexibility of doctrine, but for their professorial manner in parliamentary debate. Besides Royer-Collard and Guizot, the group also had as prominent members Camille Jordan, de Serre, de Broglie, and de Barante, with Pasquier and de Rémusat at times marginal members.

[3] See Donald Southgate, *The Passing of the Whigs, 1832–1886* (London: Macmillan, 1962), pp. 196 ff., for definition of "Whiggery."

[4] As in John Plamenatz, *The Revolutionary Movement in France, 1815–71* (London: Longmans, 1952), chaps. 2 and 3; and Réne Rémond, *La Droite en France* (Paris: Aubier Éditions, Montaigne, 1954), chap. 3.

dlingness is somewhat obscured. And more often than not
they are ridiculed rather than taken seriously. Although
Brougham and Macaulay have begun to receive more kindly
attention in recent years,[5] they have traditionally been targets
of sarcasm for critics ranging from Bagehot to Brinton. As
for the Doctrinaires, Douglas Johnson's recent and serious
study of Guizot is refreshing,[6] but still an exception in the
tradition of scorn which has surrounded the French *juste
milieu* theorists. Roger Soltau, for example, doubts that Guizot "really knew what a first principle was"—unless it was
the "supremacy of the middle class."[7] This is fully in the tradition of Henri Michel, who found "absence of principle"
the striking trait of the Doctrinaires, accused Royer-Collard
of "bargaining between fact and right, to the detriment of
right," and called Guizot "the theorist par excellence of that
which later came to be called opportunism."[8]

Although there is truth in some of this criticism, the underlying theme is hardly fair. The fact that the Doctrinaires
and Whigs idealized the middle class is no adequate reason
for dismissing their ideas out of hand as nothing more than
transparent apology for crass class interest. It is not simply
that they were concerned with the important problem of
middlingness. It is rather that they dealt with that problem
at a level of some sophistication. For their apotheosis of the
middle class and the middle position could claim a certain

[5] For example, Chester New, *The Life of Henry Peter Brougham to
1830* (Oxford: Clarendon Press, 1961); Frances Hawes, *Henry Brougham*
(London: Jonathan Cape, 1957); David Knowles, *Lord Macaulay, 1800–
1859* (Cambridge University Press, 1960); G. R. Potter, *Macaulay* (London: Longmans, 1959); Mark A. Thomson, *Macaulay* (London: Routledge
and Kegan Paul, 1959).

[6] *Guizot: Aspects of French History, 1787–1874* (London: Routledge
and Kegan Paul, 1963).

[7] *French Political Thought in the 19th Century* (Yale University Press,
1931), p. 44.

[8] *L'Idée de l'État* (Paris, 1896), pp. 292, 294.

philosophic priority. In both England and France it involved fairly elaborate, if not highly systematic, concepts of sovereignty, representation, freedom, and history. For another thing, like the problem of middlingness itself, these ideas clearly have a high degree of historical importance in terms of the emergence of the liberal-constitutional state in the early to mid-nineteenth century. By the standards of "great political thought," no one could claim the stature of a Burke or a Rousseau for the theorists of *juste milieu*. Nevertheless, these theorists did provide the immediate, operational ideas with which constitutional government was established in France and reformed in England after the Napoleonic wars.

If the commentators have neglected these theorists individually, it should not surprise that they have failed almost completely to study them *comparatively*—that is, to explore and develop the interesting correlations which exist between Whig and Doctrinaire ideas, despite the differing political and social contexts of England and France. The almost complete dearth of such comparative analysis, not the scant or unkind attention paid to this or that theorist, is the really disappointing thing about most studies of nineteenth-century European political thought. As Professor Louis Hartz has observed, "When we come to comparative dynamic analyses such as the correlation between the First Reform Act and the July Revolution, we are in a poverty-stricken area indeed."[9] Although I would not be so immodest as to claim the adjective "dynamic" for the present study, I think that its *raison d'être* should be clear from what has been said here.

Since this is a study of ideas, perhaps I should also explain briefly at the outset the sense in which I use the expression "ideology." Essentially I accept Professor Carl Friedrich's definition: "Ideologies are sets of ideas related to the existing political and social order and intended either to change it or

[9] *The Liberal Tradition in America* (New York: Harcourt, Brace, 1955), pp. 26–27.

to defend it."[10] Although Whig and Doctrinaire ideas
through the years proposed the defense of certain aspects and
the change of other aspects of the existing order, surely they
conform to that definition. I also accept Professor Friedrich's
argument that "ideologies, as action related systems of ideas,
are exposed . . . to the danger that the projected action is
palpably unrealizable."[11] However, I do not, as does he, use
the word "utopia" to describe an ideology which has become the victim of that danger. Instead, I have preferred to
use the word "unreal" to describe ideas which envision palpably unrealizable developments in the future or which are
predicated upon a palpably false view of the present. My reason has been, quite simply, to avoid any possible confusion
between the definition just stated and Karl Mannheim's celebrated typology which defines as "ideology" ideas which ra-
tionalize and defend the existing order and as "utopia" ideas
which transcend and transform that order.[12]

Having mentioned Mannheim, I should add that although
a discussion[13] of his typology has seemed to me unnecessary
to the purpose of this essay, I do comment at the conclusion
of my analysis on both his particular view of *juste milieu*
theory and his general theme of social class as the master de-
terminant of the style and content of ideas. It should be clear
from what has already been said and from what follows that
I have found *juste milieu* theory to be something rather more
subtle and complicated than a mere reflection of class interest.

Finally, I am deeply indebted and grateful to Professor
Hartz of Harvard not only for suggesting to me the topic

[10] *Man and His Government* (New York: McGraw-Hill, 1963), p. 89.
[11] *Ibid.,* p. 92.
[12] See especially *Ideology and Utopia* (New York: Harvest Books, n.d.),
passim.
[13] For such a discussion and criticism, see Carl Friedrich and Z. K.
Brzezinski, *Totalitarian Dictatorship and Autocracy* (Harvard University
Press, 1956), pp. 73 ff.

of this work but also for his continuing interest and help in every stage of its genesis. I also wish to express my appreciation for the wise counsel and encouragement of Professors Arthur Wilson, Kalman Silvert, and Henry Ehrmann of Dartmouth College and for fellowships from Dartmouth and the Social Science Research Council which greatly assisted in completion of the work. Where I have quoted English translations of French passages, I have so acknowledged in my notes. For the other translations, and indeed for all else that follows, the responsibility is mine.

Vincent E. Starzinger

Norwich, Vermont
March 1965

CONTENTS

MIDDLINGNESS

Juste Milieu *Political Theory* *in France and England, 1815–48*

First Citizen
Sir, there's a hurry in the veins of youth,
that makes a vice of virtue by excess.

Second Citizen
What if the coolness of our tardier veins
be loss of virtue?

First Citizen
All things cool with time,—the sun itself,
they say, till heat shall find a general level,
nowhere in excess.

Second Citizen
'Tis a poor climax,
to my weaker thought, that future
middlingness.

George Eliot, *Felix Holt*

Chapter One

INTRODUCTION

The View across the Channel

WHENEVER one finds similar schools of political thought in two different nations at the same time, he cannot help but wonder about the view which each has or had of the other. In a comparative study of early nineteenth-century Whig and Doctrinaire theories of middlingness, this query is especially relevant for two reasons. First, the commentators seem often to have misjudged the Whig and Doctrinaire views of each other across the Channel. Second, those views suggest at the outset some interesting insights into the kind and quality of political theory which results from commitment to the center position, and that problem is one with which this analysis of middlingness is very much concerned.

The two relations usually noted between the Doctrinaires' *juste milieu* and English Whiggism are quite limited. Looking from France to England, the commentators have often observed that the Doctrinaires felt a general affinity for the Whigs, were close students of English constitutional development, and were seemingly guilty of trying to copy English institutions.[1] Yet if one takes the Doctrinaires' own professions at face value, it was England's Glorious Revolution of 1688 and not the Great Reform Bill with which they

[1] Soltau, *op. cit.,* pp. 34–35, 58; J. P. Mayer, *Political Thought in France* (London: Routledge and Kegan Paul, 1949), pp. 9 ff. On arriving in England in 1840 as ambassador to the Court of St. James, Guizot noted that he found himself "already in mutual and somewhat intimate relations" with the Whigs. For one thing, compared with the Tories, the Whigs "had more taste for . . . French ideas and manners" (Guizot, *Embassy to St. James* [London, 1862], p. 126).

seemed to equate the July Revolution. Their critics have usually been content to accept the 1688–1830 identification and let the matter drop.[2] To do this, however, is not quite enough. For whatever the Doctrinaires' professions, there is in fact a clear but seldom drawn analogy between the basic ideas of the French *juste milieu* and those of Whiggism in the Reform Bill era. And the analogy is not limited to a general preoccupation with middlingness and eulogies of the middle class. It also includes concepts of sovereignty, representation, freedom, and history. Although the precise terms in which the two groups articulated these ideas varied somewhat, the underlying correlation is still striking enough to suggest that the Doctrinaires were, consciously or not, identifying France with contemporary England, and their own position with that of the Whigs. If this tacit identification seems hypothetical at this point, it will become far less so as we go along.

The view across the Channel in the other direction is less speculative. The traditional interpretation has been that the news of the July Revolution, arriving in England at the beginning of the general elections of 1830, turned the country strongly against the Tory ministry and stoked the fires of reform for the great battle of 1831–32. Emphasized by Halévy,[3] this view has considerable contemporary support.

[2] Guizot, *Mémoires pour Servir à l'Histoire de Mon Temps* (Paris, 1858–61), II, 18 ff.; Duvergier de Hauranne, *Histoire du Gouvernement Parlementaire en France, 1814–48* (Paris, 1871), X, 402 ff. See also E. L. Woodward, *Three Studies in European Conservatism* (London: Constable, 1929), p. 141; Soltau, *op. cit.,* p. 35; Guido de Ruggiero, *History of European Liberalism,* trans. R. G. Collingwood (Oxford University Press, 1927), p. 176. Although Douglas Johnson, *op. cit.,* pp. 22, 52, 61, 438, takes passing notice of Guizot's "Victorian" traits, the Doctrinaires' interest in the *Edinburgh Review,* the similarity of "parliamentary life" in England and France at the time, and the pan-European appeal of "Whiggery," he fails to develop the analogy suggested here.

[3] Elie Halévy, *History of the English People in the 19th Century* (London: Ernest Benn, 1950), III, 3 ff.; also J. R. M. Butler, *The Passing of the Great Reform Bill* (London: Longmans, 1914), p. 85.

For example, Francis Place, the "Radical Tailor of Charing Cross," described the effect of the July news in England as "extraordinary."[4] Wellington himself felt that the elections of 1830 would have been another Tory victory "if the French Revolution had not occurred at the very moment of the dissolution of Parliament."[5] Perhaps, however, such judgments about electoral results have been taken too much at face value. For example, Norman Gash has recently managed to cast a fairly heavy cloud over the Halévy thesis. After determining the large number of uncontested constituencies in 1830 and the number already decided before the news from Paris, as well as examining campaign speeches in other selected contests, Gash has concluded that the July Revolution was at most "an accidental and superficial feature" of the elections which ended a generation of Tory rule.[6]

In any event, whether the events in France in 1830 helped in some direct fashion to put Earl Grey's Whig ministry in power is not vitally relevant to the broad analogy of ideas with which I am concerned. And, interestingly enough, when one explores more generally the English view of France he finds a far more explicit awareness of this analogy than on the other side of the Channel. Not only did the Reform Whigs clearly sense the affinity between their own and Doctrinaire theory, but for a good many years before and after 1830 they also either implied or insisted that their strategic political position in England was directly analogous to the Doctrinaires' in France. Although in later years most Whigs were to have a more perceptive understanding of the real differences between French and English politics, this earlier view was significant background for the formulation

---

[4] Quoted in Graham Wallas, *The Life of Francis Place* (London: Unwin, 1918), p. 244.

[5] Quoted, by permission of Macmillan & Co., Ltd., from Norman Gash, "English Reform and French Revolution in the General Election of 1830," R. Pares and A. J. P. Taylor, ed., *Essays Presented to Sir Lewis Namier* (London: Macmillan, 1956), pp. 258–59.   [6] *Ibid.,* p. 288.

of their ideas in the era of reform. Yet it is background which Halévy really did not develop, and which Gash seems to deny. Granting that the extremists in English politics "were prepared to draw [contemporary] analogies," Gash declares:

> United as Englishmen were in welcoming the revolution (of 1830), however, they were not necessarily conscious of any need to extract from the scenes enacted in France a lesson for their own political behavior. . . . The analogy that presented itself most strongly to the ordinary English mind was between 1830 and 1688. What England had achieved a century and a half ago, France was now after a long interval endeavoring to emulate.
>
> . . . . .
>
> Englishmen of *moderate* views . . . were prepared to admit defects in their constitution and wished to have them reformed; *but they could not see that there was any essential similarity between the political situation in France and in England.*[7]

In answer to Gash I would submit the following passage from the *Edinburgh Review,* surely a voice of "moderate" political thought:

> The cause of peace in Europe and of good government in France is staked on the stability of the throne of Louis Philippe. *The intermediate position which his government has taken up between two irreconcilable extremes, is precisely identical with the intermediate position at present occupied by the administration of Earl Grey.*[8]

This article, a review of M. Sarrans' *Lafayette and the Revolution of 1830,* goes on to draw a direct analogy between the

---

[7] *Ibid.,* pp. 263, 268–70 (italics mine).
[8] LVI (Jan. 1833), 487 (italics mine)

recent "disturbances at Lyons" and "our Bristol riots or stack yard burnings." France's three great parties are even identified as "its Tory Carlists, its *juste milieu* Whigs, and its Radical Republicans." François Guizot and the Duc de Broglie are praised as "always the tried and consistent friends of freedom . . . the most accomplished scholars . . . of constitutional learning."[9]

The reason for this extravagant praise is clear when the *Review* explains the Whigs' "intermediate position" in almost the same terms which we will find the Doctrinaires using in rationalizing their "golden mean" between the extremes of Ancien Regime and Revolution. The Whig regime exists "only under the pledge of reconciling liberty and order." "Order is worth little without liberty; but liberty is worth nothing without order."[10] The *Review* obviously has Grey as well as Guizot in mind in defending the latter:

M. Guizot has been gibbetted with every mark of extravagant obloquy by the Republicans of France. And why? Simply because he has endeavored to weave into a piece, on the safest and most honourable terms, the past, the present, and the future destinies of his country, and to consolidate . . . a monarchical executive, with a republican legislative control.[11]

Finally, the *Review* complains about the same irresponsible *ad hoc* coalitions of extremists which plagued the Doctrinaires' center position in France:

On both sides of the Channel, the enemies of liberty and . . . of order make common cause against the actual governments of France and England. Mr. Sarrans pelts the Doctrinaires with the reproofs of M. Polignac. So our con-

---

[9] *Ibid.*, 489, 491–92.   [10] *Ibid.*, 482, 485.   [11] *Ibid.*, 492.

servative provincials quote the *Standard* in one column and the *Examiner* in the next.[12]

The Whig sense of kinship with the French *juste milieu* was no passing affair. Throughout his life Lord Russell referred approvingly to the Doctrinaires as "French Whigs."[13] In 1819 the *Edinburgh Review* was already commending de Broglie as an eminent founder of "rational liberty" in France.[14] Discussing English electoral reform a year later, the *Review* gave its explicit endorsement to the Doctrinaires' theory of representation.[15] Again, in 1826, the ideas of the Doctrinaires were praised for "a clearness and strength of argument, a range and depth of views which but few of our Noble thinkers could rival."[16] Guizot's various histories invariably drew special eulogy for his statesmanship—e.g., for the "systematic consistency of his whole political life, which . . . gave the authority of a minister to the principles of a philosopher."[17]

This affinity for the Doctrinaires reflected the Whigs' continuing emphasis on their own intermediate position in English politics. As early as 1810 Francis Jeffrey had declared:

The great body of the nation appears to us to be divided into two violent and most pernicious factions;—the courtiers, who are almost for arbitrary power;—and the democrats, who are almost for revolution and republicanism. Between these stand a small, but most respectable band—the friends

[12] *Ibid.*, 482. This was a recurring Whig complaint. See also *Edinburgh Review*, LVIII (Jan. 1834), 457; T. B. Macaulay, *Miscellanies* (Boston: Houghton Mifflin, 1900), I, 29–30 (speech in House of Commons, July 5, 1831).
[13] John Earl Russell, *Recollections and Suggestions, 1813–73* (London: Longmans, 1875), p. 448.
[14] XXXII (July 1819), 192–93.   [15] *Ibid.*, XXXIV (Aug. 1820), 38.
[16] *Ibid.*, XLIV (June 1826), 156.
[17] *Ibid.*, CVIII (Oct. 1858), 410. See also LXVII (July 1838), 357 ff., and LXXXII (Oct. 1845), 381 ff.

of liberty and order—the Old Constitutional Whigs of England.[18]

In 1826 Jeffrey repeated this same middling theme:

> If there were no natural war between Democracy and Monarchy, no true ground of discord between Tories and Radical reformers—we admit there would be no vocation for Whigs: for the true definition of that party . . . is that it is a middle party, between the two extremes of high monarchical principles . . . and extremely popular principles.[19]

Ten years later the *Edinburgh Review* still had the same view of a "chasm in English society," with the two extreme parties standing "like cliffs that have been rent asunder." Only the Whigs' "central post" kept the extremes from "rushing into immediate and fierce collision."[20]

During the height of the English battle for parliamentary reform, the favorite Whig reference to France was to equate Tory with Ultra. In 1824 Henry Peter Brougham had already written a long, sarcastic description of Charles X's new reign with the expressed hope that the Tories, blind to their own follies at home, might possibly recognize them in another setting.[21] In 1830 he called the July Revolution "a fatal warning held out to our rulers."[22] Wellington was a frequent butt of the French analogy. When the Duke refused to countenance parliamentary reform, the *Edinburgh Review* declared, "except for . . . Prince Polignac, no public man ever yet exhibited such strange defiance of common sense and public opinion."[23] Antireformers were now referred to

---

[18] *Ibid.*, XV (Jan. 1810), 504. [19] *Ibid.*, XLV (Dec. 1826), 35.

[20] *Ibid.*, LXV (July 1837), 267–69.

[21] Henry Peter Brougham, *Contributions to the Edinburgh Review* (London, 1856), II, 506 ff.

[22] In the *Edinburgh Review,* LII (Oct. 1830), 12. See New, *op. cit.,* pp. 419 ff., for appendix concerning Brougham's authorship of articles in the *Review*.

[23] LII (Jan. 1831), 531.

as the "tyrants of July,"[24] and when the House of Lords threatened to block the Reform Bill, the *Review* asked, "Who will be the British Polignac?"[25] Fortunately the question never had to be answered. But had a British Polignac appeared, Brougham, for one, apparently would not have shirked what he considered the logic of the French parallel. As he wrote his friend de Broglie:

> I know we shall now follow your glorious example, if—which God avert—it should ever become necessary. The promptitude shown by the Parisians in resisting; their sagacity in feeling . . . that it was a case for arms, and not for courts of law; but more than all, their signal temperance, and even humanity, in victory—are the finest lesson to other countries that any people ever afforded in any age.[26]

If this sketch has documented the Whigs' affinity for the Doctrinaires and their willingness to draw analogy between contemporary French and English politics, perhaps we should note briefly the Tory and Radical views. The Tories professed to regard the Whigs not as a "middle party," but as "traitors to their order" who were really engaged in "revolution under the name of reform."[27] The "French Whigs" were viewed no more kindly. In May 1830 the *Quarterly Review* hoped that Charles X and Prince Polignac would survive mounting liberal attacks even if press censorship and abolition of the Charter of 1814 were needed.[28] Five months later the *Review* temporized somewhat by observing, "Charles X, having been wholly in the right, managed to put himself wholly in the wrong." But the Tory organ made it quite clear that Charles' chief misdeed was simply to have "miscalcu-

---

[24] *Ibid.*, LIII (June 1831), 497.   [25] *Ibid.*, LIV (Sept. 1831), 274.

[26] Brougham, *Life and Times* (New York: Harper Bros., 1872), III, 46.

[27] Lord Eldon's phrase, quoted in Horace Twiss, *Life of Lord Eldon, With Selections from His Correspondence* (Philadelphia: Carey and Hart, 1844), II, 233.

[28] XLIII (May 1830), 239.

lated his strength."[29] Finally, with Whigs in power in both France and England, one Tory pamphleteer scored the Whig-Doctrinaire correlation in these provocative terms: "So far from the French being such fools as to imitate us, they have run a far wiser course, and our new Government, taking the recommendation of the *Edinburgh Review,* are pulling ours to pieces to rebuild it on the last French model.[30]

On the opposite flank the English Radicals also exploited the Whig-Doctrinaire comparison, but in quite a different sense. Far from being agents of revolution, Whigs on both sides of the Channel only pretended liberalism, while still serving the old aristocratic order. The *Westminster Review* dismissed the Whig-Tory and Doctrinaire-Legitimist distinctions as matters largely of "accident" or parliamentary "strategy."[31] France's new *juste milieu* Charter of 1830 was "a trick from the beginning" and Pierre Paul Royer-Collard simply an "old correspondent of the emigrants and intimate of the plots of Louis XVIII."[32] Although the July Revolution was "carried through from dread and horror of having something like the constitution of the English borough-holders imposed" on France, the new Orleanist regime had betrayed rather than fulfilled the Revolution.[33] The *juste milieu* was government by a "privileged class" whose leaders demonstrated "incapacity, selfishness, and bad faith," and whose only achievement was "sham liberty."[34]

Despite their alliance with the Whigs during the Reform Bill battle, the Radicals represented by the *Westminster Review* feared in England exactly the same betrayal of liberty which they claimed to see in *juste milieu* France. From its

[29] *Ibid.,* XLIII (Oct. 1830), 596.

[30] John Eagles, *The Bristol Riots* (Bristol, 1832), pp. 17–18.

[31] I (Jan. 1824), 206, 210–19; XV (Oct. 1831), 418–19; XVII (Oct. 1832), 432.

[32] *Ibid.,* XVII (July 1832), 213, 222. [33] *Ibid.,* XIV (April 1831), 444.

[34] *Ibid.,* XV (Oct. 1831), 424, 431; XVII (Oct. 1832), 432.

93397

first issues the *Review* had castigated the Whigs' strategy of "see-sawing" and "trimming" on every conceivable issue in order "to gain favor from both the few and the many." In the *Review*'s judgment, this practice not only sacrificed truth to convenience but invariably betrayed the interests of the people to those of the aristocracy. The Whig secret was "being ingenious in the invention of schemes . . . which may have the appearance to the people of being calculated to add to their securities, but which would, even if accomplished, leave the power of the aristocracy untouched."[35] No wonder, then, that almost as soon as the Reform Bill had passed, the *Review* began asking if "the English will be cheated like the French in July? . . . No frauds of the *juste milieu* here. The example is providential."[36]

At this point it is unnecessary to belabor the fact that underlying political realities in England and France hardly conformed to this insistence on a direct, unequivocal analogy between the Whig and Doctrinaire strategic positions. Despite the dark days of disorder after Waterloo, the menacing masses of Chartism, and the presence of Ultras on the right as well as the left, England simply did not face in the nineteenth century the same range of political extremism and disintegration that France did. If England had had her Glorious Revolution, it had hardly been the cataclysm of France's 1789. In turn, the Whig settlement of 1832 was a pacific "reform," not a "revolution" in even the mild sense of the July Days in Paris. Although observers at the time and since have compared the Bristol riots of 1831 with the insurrection of silk workers in the same year at Lyons, there were significant differences in the nature of even these two outbreaks of violence, as well as in the measures taken to quell them.

Most importantly of all, the two *justes milieux* met radically different political fates. The French *juste milieu*, ration-

[35] *Ibid.*, I (Jan. 1824), 221.   [36] *Ibid.*, XVII (July 1832), 254.

alized by the Doctrinaires during the Restoration and then institutionalized by the July Revolution, inexorably particularized itself into the narrow, inflexible regime of the 1840s, while the English *juste milieu* proved a vital, expanding center. True, the Whigs as a party did not survive the emergence of mass democracy and the problems of maturing industrialism in the later nineteenth century. It may also be that from hindsight one can trace the "passing" of the Whigs back to a failure in earlier decades to transcend their aristocratic origins and exploit fully the success of the 1832 settlement.[37] Nevertheless, the fact remains that the *juste milieu* terms of that settlement proved eminently viable, lasting the full thirty-five years—"an eternity in politics"—which Sidney Smith had predicted.[38] Even after mid-century, those who agitated for further extension of the franchise were embarrassed by the apathy of the nation toward that issue.[39] In sum, if the Doctrinaires' experiment in middlingness ended with the catastrophe of revolution in February and June of 1848, that same year brought in England the final, pathetic fizzle of Chartism and seemed to underwrite for the future the smug Whig assumption that 1832 was indeed a "permanent solution."

It is also unnecessary at this point to detail the significant societal factors which underlay these differing political patterns. It should suffice here to say that the social structures of the two nations—especially the English middle class and the French bourgeoisie—were hardly counterparts. Not only were the two nations at rather different physical stages of industrial development; in a deeper sense, France was continuingly ambivalent toward the middle-class, commercial-industrial values which had such wide currency in England.

[37] See Southgate, *op. cit., passim,* for an elaborate treatment of this thesis.
[38] Quoted in Butler, *op. cit.,* p. 256.   [39] Southgate, *op. cit.,* p. 304.

To say that England was not France, however, does not make a study of Whig and Doctrinaire theory meaningless. For one thing, we have still to *explain* the Whig and Doctrinaire views across the Channel. Even more importantly, the fact remains that the Great Reform and the July Revolution did institutionalize remarkably similar *theories* of middle class *juste milieu* rule. The contrast of politics and society on opposite sides of the Channel *plus* that analogy of ideas are precisely what make these two experiments in middlingness fascinating to explore.

The Character of Juste Milieu *Ideology*

To return to the views across the Channel, the tendency to mistake France for England, and vice versa, reveals some important characteristics of *juste milieu* theory qua theory. One of these characteristics is the curious strain of unreality which runs through Whig and Doctrinaire thought. When we turn to substantive ideas like sovereignty and representation, this strain will be more impressive on the French than the English side of the Channel. But as their explicit identification of England with France suggests, even the Whigs did not escape it. True, the precise terms in which the two schools cast their ideas differ interestingly, in either conscious or unconscious response to the differing environments in which they were operating. But if *juste milieu* theory seems on occasion to confirm the old cliché that political ideas mirror social reality in some direct fashion, it also suggests that ideas can just as often be a dream fantasy of what is *not* social reality. And by "dream" I do not mean "aspiration" in the sense of ideas which attempt to transcend and transform society on the basis of a clear distinction between what "is" and what "ought to be." I mean instead a kind of unwitting self-deception which either refuses to face or egregiously miscalculates the historical reality of the present. The more one ponders *juste milieu* political theory the more one is struck by the important part which such "sincere masquerade"[40] can play in political ideology. Yet it is a part of ideology which goes largely unnoticed in such overly rationalistic views as the conventional judgment that Whig and Doctrinaire ideas were nothing more than a reflection of blatant class interest.

Perhaps, however, I am begging the question. Is it possible that these apparent flights from reality were nothing more than knowing deceits practiced for partisan advantage? There are, I would submit, several objections to this argument. Take the case of the Whig insistence on the direct analogy of English and French political positions. It is true that the Whigs—or most of them—survived this error with relative impunity, perhaps even advantage, and the error may well have involved some partisan rhetoric. But to dismiss the theme of analogy in these terms simply does not square with either its frequent reiteration by all three English parties or the plausibility which it must have seemed to have in the rush of events.[41] Whatever hindsight may tell, one could understandably have mistaken England for France in moments of exigency like the Peterloo massacre, the Bristol riots, and the Chartist marches. As for the even more serious discrepancies between Doctrinaire ideas and political reality, including the seemingly tacit identification with England, fate was far less

---

[40] Irving Howe's phrase, *Politics and the Novel* (New York: Horizon Press, 1957), p. 71.

[41] For an argument that the Millite Radicals deliberately exaggerated the danger of imminent revolution in England in order to convince the Whigs that the Reform Bill of 1832 was a necessary concession, see Joseph Hamburger, *James Mill and the Art of Revolution* (Yale University Press, 1963), *passim*. Since the Whigs themselves held their own unreal image of English politics for a good many years before and after 1832, the Radical strategy would hardly seem to be the basic source of the image. For further comment on Hamburger, see below, pp. 49–50.

CALVIN T. RYAN LIBRARY
KEARNEY STATE COLLEGE
KEARNEY, NEBRASKA

kind with the French *juste milieu* than the English. Far from proving "opportunistic," Doctrinaire miscalculations and dream turned out to be disastrous.

Another objection to the opportunistic view of *juste milieu* theory is a bit more speculative. Grant that extremist political thought is itself often unrealistic, there may be something about the nature of the center position per se which inclines it also to theorize in unreal terms, despite the perennial claim of the middling mind to understand practical necessity. First, a left or right position need calculate danger on only one front. That is usually difficult enough. But the risk of miscalculation may well be compounded for a center position simply because it is exposed on two fronts. In turn, any strategic misjudgments are likely to be reflected in the ideas with which the center rationalizes its position.

A second, more subtle trap in which the middling mind may be caught involves the relation between consensus in a political system and commitment to the center. The society rent between two massive political extremes is obviously the most relevant context for a theory of middlingness. But that context is also precisely where the center is least realistic—in the sense that the *juste milieu* call of reasonableness will probably go unheard and that the center will very likely be pulverized from both sides and driven to futile negativism. On the other hand, commitment to the center is likely to be a fairly realistic enterprise where the political left and right both stand within the same value consensus. Yet this latter context may well be one in which it is irrelevant to insist on the middle way. After all, the more moderate the left and right are themselves, the less point there is to be preoccupied with avoiding extremes. *One might say, then, that the center is least realistic where it is most relevant, and most realistic where it is least relevant.*

As a result of this curious trap the middling mind, without quite realizing it, seems often to be faced with one or the other of two temptations. In the first instance, where mid-dlingness is eminently relevant but unrealistic, the tempta-tion is to exaggerate the power of sweet reasonableness. In the second instance, where middlingness is realistic but irrele-vant, the middling mind seems easily tempted to conjure up as its *raison d'être* the specter of intransigent adversaries on either side. This attempt to be both realistic and relevant at the same time may be no slight clue to the Whig insistence that the English extremes were directly analogous to the French, and to the Doctrinaires' tacit identification of France with England. In the case of the Whigs the exaggeration of extremes made an already realistic center seem even more relevant than it was. In the case of the Doctrinaires, to mis-take France for England was to attribute to France a reasona-bleness in politics which would make the *juste milieu* a realistic as well as relevant center. Obviously, however, com-parisons across the Channel, whether they added an aura of realism or relevance to the *juste milieu,* were themselves flights to unreality.

However speculative this realism-relevance suggestion may be, perhaps I have unwittingly undercut my earlier argument that the Whigs and Doctrinaires were themselves unwitting in their miscalculations. If they were in fact fol-lowing the strategy which I have suggested, did they realize it? Probably any answer would be a guess. My guess is that the response of the middling mind to the realism-relevance problem is more often than not unconscious. It is more a reflex function of middlingness than a deliberate intellectual process. But even if this guess is completely wrong, the phe-nomenon which I have described is still a far more delicate, subtle order of deceit than the critics usually have had in mind when accusing the *juste milieu* theorists of opportun-ism. In any event, we will soon see more of it.

Another characteristic of *juste milieu* theory is that the center position in politics can seldom deny at least some ideological legitimacy to the extremes which it confronts. Granted that the initial choice of the center may involve a certain philosophic priority, the position itself has a significant impact—in addition to that already noted—on the substance of the ideas with which it is rationalized. For after all, a middle point or mean is itself a *derivative* of whatever extremes exist. The usual response of *juste milieu* theory is therefore not to reject absolutely the values of the extremes, but rather to moderate those values in a synthesis of categories from left and right. The result is that the extremes often hold, from first to last, a crucial initiative in determining the categories of ideological dispute. The *Edinburgh Review* admitted as much—in fact, overstated the point—when it defined Whiggism's commitment to middlingness and declared:

It holds no peculiar opinions, that we are aware of, on any other points of policy,—and no man of common sense can doubt that . . . it differs from each of the other parties on the very grounds on which they differ from each other,—the only distinction being that it does not differ so widely.[42]

"Positional ideology" is the phrase which Samuel Huntington has suggested to distinguish this kind of political theory from other ideology which he calls "inherent." By this typology, an inherent ideology is the "theoretical expression of the interests of a continuing social group." The independent identity of the group yields an ideology of rationally related concepts which themselves have continuing validity to the group regardless of its strategic position in the political spectrum. Positional ideologies, however, "do not reflect the continuing interests and needs of a particular social group. Rather they depend upon the relations among groups." That is, they are "functions of situations no matter what groups occupy those situations. With positional ideologies, it is a

[42] XLV (Dec. 1826), 35.

question not of 'who' but of 'where.' " Although Huntington is concerned with applying these categories to conservatism in general, he does, interestingly enough, mention both Royer-Collard and Guizot as "positionally" determined theorists.[43]

If this suggests that his typology might well be useful in a more detailed study of *juste milieu* theory, one word of warning is in order at the outset: quite obviously the definitions of "positional" and "inherent" do not set up an either-or dichotomy. For Whig and Doctrinaire ideas would clearly seem to involve some question of "who" as well as "where." The middle-class theme is far too persistent for *juste milieu* theory to be labeled exclusively positional. Even Huntington trips over this problem in a self-contradiction. For having called the Doctrinaires positional theorists, what does he then select as his first example of a group possessing an inherent ideology? It is none other than the very "bourgeois middle class" of which Royer-Collard and Guizot were archtheorists! Moreover, despite the *Edinburgh Review*'s modesty, the Whigs and Doctrinaires did elaborate the middle-class theme with some political concepts which could fairly be called their own. Nevertheless, if cautiously used, the positional-inherent distinction can be helpful in understanding the interplay of factors which make *juste milieu* ideology so elusive in nature.

[43] "Conservatism as an Ideology," *American Political Science Review,* LI (June 1957), 466–68.

Chapter Two

THE SOVEREIGNTY OF REASON

AND THE MIXED STATE

Two Routes to Reason

THE Doctrinaires' concept of sovereignty was a direct corollary of their view of the Great Revolution. Guizot and Royer-Collard neither rejected nor accepted the Revolution en bloc. This was surely a matter of personal experience, as well as theory. After being a member of the Convention in 1793, Royer-Collard himself had later had a narrow escape during the Terror, and Guizot had lost his father to the guillotine.[1] For Guizot the excesses of the Revolution were essentially the result of a disastrous moral mistake: the belief that man was naturally good, or, rather, that institutions were the sole source of evil.[2] True, he welcomed the end of feudal privileges and was convinced that the "principles and acts of 1789 produced, within civil society, the essential reforms."[3] Yet he never tired of arguing that the "spirit of revolution," however necessary at certain moments, is generally poison to both liberty and order.[4] Royer-Collard shared these same views, reserving the right to judge the Revolution "as severely as is proper and as justice demands."[5]

Justice demanded an even more severe verdict against the Ancien Regime. By Guizot's definition, the task of the Restoration was "to establish constitutional order and resist the

---

[1] E. Spuller, *Royer-Collard* (Paris, 1895), pp. 29–30; Mme. Guizot-de Witt, *The Private Life of Guizot* (Boston: Estes & Lauriat, 1882), pp. 2–3.

[2] Guizot, *Histoire Parlementaire de France* (Paris, 1863), I, xxii–xxiii.

[3] *Mémoires*, VIII, 540.

[4] *Histoire Parlementaire*, I, 176–77, 321; III, 153.

[5] Baron P. de Barante, *La Vie Politique de M. Royer-Collard, Ses Discours et Ses Écrits* (Paris, 1861), II, 104.

Ancien Regime."[6] Royer-Collard admonished the Chamber of Deputies: "I do not consider the counterrevolution good or lawful in any part."[7] The great services of the French nobility in past ages were now no more than "souvenirs de l'histoire" and the Bourbon monarchy which had returned to France after Napoleon's fall must be regarded as a "new monarchy, separated from the old by events which are as centuries."[8]

The sovereignty of "reason" and "justice" was the basic philosophic concept with which the Doctrinaires rejected the exclusive claims of either the Revolution or the Ancien Regime. Essentially that concept was a denial of the traditional notion of sovereignty. By that I mean a denial that within any polity there must somewhere be an ultimate, absolute, institutional point of authority. Royer-Collard appealed from the sovereignty of óne person, of an assembly, or of all, to "another sovereignty, the only one which merits that name, a sovereignty superior to peoples as to kings, a sovereignty as immutable and immortal as is its source, I mean the sovereignty of reason."[9] This was also a frequent theme with Guizot.[10] Discarding Montesquieu's conventional classification of governments, Guizot insisted that the true classification depended on whether sovereignty was vested in human agency or in reason and justice. Of these two forms, only the latter could claim legitimacy. Governments which "attribute sovereignty as a right belonging exclusively to individuals, whether one, many, or all those combining a society . . . are, in principle, the founders of despotism. . . . The second class of governments is founded upon the truth that sovereignty belongs as a right to no individual whatever,

[6] *Des Moyens de Gouvernement et d'Opposition* (Paris, 1821), p. 2.

[7] Barante, *op. cit.,* II, 104.

[8] *Ibid.,* p. 184. (See also Robert de Nesmes-Desmarets, *Les Doctrines Politiques de Royer-Collard* [Paris, 1908], p. 67.)

[9] Barante, *op. cit.,* II, 459.

[10] *Du Gouvernement de la France depuis la Restauration* (Paris, 1821), pp. 201 ff.; also his 1826 essay "Élections" in *Discours Académiques* (Paris, 1862), p. 406.

since the perfect and continued application of justice and reason do not belong to our imperfect nature."[11] This same fear of tyranny underlay Royer-Collard's sovereignty of reason: the Ancien Regime's claim of royal sovereignty led to a "simple despotism," the Revolution's claim of popular sovereignty to a "composite despotism."[12]

Although its positional overtones are obvious, this concept of sovereignty was clearly a rather ingenious theoretical tactic and innovation. Georges Burdeau has argued that it entitles Guizot "to be considered one of the founders, in France, of the liberal state."[13] Even a person as skeptical of liberalism as Harold Laski could see in Royer-Collard's statement of the doctrine the primitive outlines of modern pluralism.[14]

Both these compliments go to the heart of an important problem of modern constitutionalism: reconciling the traditional notion of sovereignty with the actual dispersal of power and decision-making centers in a pluralized political system. Although the Doctrinaires' solution was hardly definitive, it was rather less clumsy than many other attempts have been—for example, the circuitous route by which we will find the Whigs reaching much the same result or more recent definitions of sovereignty in terms of a polity's "constitution."[15] Indeed, it is hardly fair to claim, as did Michel and Faguet, that the Doctrinaires meant only to equate sovereignty with the "ensemble" of King, Peers, and Deputies, or with law and the Charter.[16] For Royer-Collard explicitly

[11] Guizot, *History of the Origins of Representative Government in Europe,* trans. Andrew R. Scoble (London: H. G. Bohn, 1861), p. 61.

[12] Barante, *op. cit.,* II, 132; see also pp. 33, 463.

[13] *Traité de Science Politique* (Paris: Librairie Générale de Droit et de Jurisprudence, R. Pichon et R. Durand-Auzias, 1953), V, 410.

[14] "Royer-Collard," *Authority in the Modern State* (Yale University Press, 1919), pp. 303–305.

[15] For example, A. D. Lindsay, *The Modern Democratic State* (Oxford University Press, 1943), pp. 213 ff.

[16] Émile Faguet, *Politiques et Moralistes du Dix-Neuvième Siècle* (Paris, 1891), I, 262, 332; Michel, *op. cit.,* p. 294.

distinguished the sovereignty of "reason" and "justice" from its exercise by governmental powers, and he also separated "justice" from mere "law." Quoting Jacques Bossuet, he declared obedience not due "a law which contradicts morality."[17] Actually, the Doctrinaires' premise was that the idea or existence of any institutional sovereign is really incompatible with constitutionalism.[18] That granted, presumably the very word "sovereignty" becomes virtually irrelevant in any theory of constitutionalism. But despite this implication[19] the Doctrinaires stopped short of that conclusion. Instead they retained sovereignty as a category of political theory, but simply emptied it of all past meaning.

In criticizing the Doctrinaires' theory of the sovereignty of reason, it is well to note that they failed to develop its external implications in terms of the sovereignty of the French nation vis à vis other nations. Like their contemporary Whigs in England, they were so preoccupied with the domestic forces of revolution and reaction that they seemed to think only in terms of the internal significance of sovereignty. That is something of a disappointment. For after all, the concepts of both monarchical and popular sovereignty were historically concomitants of the emergence of the nation-state, and the militant idea of national sovereignty followed from the fact of the nation-state. One cannot help wondering whether the Doctrinaires would have been willing explicitly to strip France as a nation of sovereignty in the same sense that they did her institutions of government. But given the circumstances of the post-Napoleonic era, it is understandable that they did not concern themselves with that further theoretical step.

[17] Barante, *op. cit.,* II, 216; Nesmes-Desmarets, *op. cit.,* pp. 62–63.

[18] For an explicit argument to this effect, see Carl J. Friedrich, *Constitutional Government and Democracy* (Boston: Ginn, 1950), p. 19.

[19] Charles E. Merriam developed this point in *History of the Theory of Sovereignty since Rousseau* (Columbia University Press, 1900), Part 4, pp. 76–79.

What is less understandable and more disconcerting is that even in their preoccupation with the establishment of domestic order, they failed to provide any rigorous, consistent definition of "reason." Sovereignty's new content proved more than a little ambiguous. At times it seemed to approach the ideas of Plato or the theocracy of a Bonald. If Royer-Collard quoted Bossuet, he also referred on another occasion to his theory of representative government, derived in large measure from the sovereignty of reason, as "cette belle théorie de Platon en action."[20] As for Guizot, his concept of sovereignty undoubtedly reflected the influence of Christian theology and his belief that an essential attribute of human existence is man's instinctive search for God.[21] In that light it could almost have been Vicomte de Bonald speaking when he declared, "The true law of man is not the work of man; he receives but does not create it; even when he submits to it, it is not his own—it is above and beyond him." Again, in any human situation there is "always . . . a truth to be discovered, a law of reason to be applied." And since ultimately "there is but one truth, one justice, so there can be but one legitimate sovereignty."[22]

But far more often Guizot spoke in terms of a less abstract, more limited "reason." Although man might bear "within himself certain notions of order, of justice, of reason," Guizot was at the same time deeply imbued with a Christian pessimism about human nature. This, after all, was the basis for his fear of any absolute power. Man's awareness and application of the law above him were always suspect. Even a sovereignty of the "intellect"—"the real sovereign of the eighteenth century"—led to tyranny. For like every other form of power, human intellect bore "a natural vice, a prin-

[20] Barante, *op. cit.,* II, 465.

[21] Johnson, *op. cit.,* pp. 38 ff., 383, 400, develops this same point.

[22] *History of Representative Government,* p. 60; *History of Civilization in Europe* (New York: Appleton, 1838), pp. 218, 220.

ciple of feebleness and abuse."[23] The "earthly reason" with
which we attempt to grasp "transcendent reason" is every-
where fallible. As Charles Pouthas put it, Guizot's view of
man's reason was neither Kantian nor utilitarian. Rather,
"this Reason, mistress of the world, is that which a Protestant
conceives, a principle of reasonableness and not of rational-
ism."[24] And like every other category of Doctrinaire theory,
"reasonableness" meant essentially the avoidance of extremes. Along with the Christian view of man, one can almost find a kind of common-law idea of the "reasonable
man": the man whose prudence consists simply of shunning
excesses.

These two notions of reason are implicit in Guizot's dis-
missal of Rousseau's social contract theory as an "absurdity."
Guizot insisted that the ideas of society and government were
inseparable. "Society without government is no more possible than government without society."[25] Why? Quite simply
because the norms of transcendent reason which bind men to
one another, making them "social" creatures, are the same
norms which any legitimate government must accept as sovereign. "Constitutional government is social sovereignty in
organized form."[26] Beyond a legitimate government there is
no extraordinary constituent power to which appeal can
justly be made. And given the fallibility of human reason,
man's realization through any government of ultimate justice can come only from "a majority . . . which counts itself
by generations." Although Guizot's faith in progress would
probably have seemed somewhat extravagant to Burke, these
words seem to echo him. "Civilization passes from genera-

[23] *Ibid.,* pp. 68, 344–45; also his *History of Representative Government,*
p. 2.
[24] Charles H. Pouthas, *Guizot pendant la Restauration* (Paris, 1923),
pp. 318 ff.
[25] *History of Representative Government,* pp. 57–58.
[26] *Mémoires,* VII, 26–27. See also Pouthas, *op. cit.,* pp. 319 ff., for
references to Guizot's unpublished essay, "Philosophie Politique."

tion to generation as a trust which each receives, with a
certain dependence, in the state in which our forefathers have
left it, in order to improve it in turn and transmit it to
posterity."[27]

Against this background it is understandable—at least in
a theoretical sense—that the Doctrinaires romanticized the
Charter of 1814 which Louis XVIII had "granted" the
French nation. For in its repudiation of the excesses of both
the Revolution and the Ancien Regime, and its consecration
of the legitimate claims of both, the Charter must have
seemed a plausible testament of the sovereignty of reason. It
declared all citizens "equal before the law," guaranteed "individual" and "religious" liberty, held property "inviolable,"
and underwrote freedom of the press subject to laws necessary to "repress abuses." In the new mixed state of the
Charter, the legislative power was to be exercised "collec-
tively" by the King, the hereditary Chamber of Peers, and
the Chamber of Deputies. The lower chamber was to be
elected, one-fifth annually, by citizens over thirty years of
age paying a direct tax of at least 300 francs yearly. The King
held the exclusive right to initiate legislation, could dissolve
the chambers, and was vested with what later proved to be
rather formidable "emergency powers."[28]

In his celebrated eulogy of the Charter, Royer-Collard
obviously saw this new polity as a transcendence of all
France's recent ordeals:

There are, then, for the institutions of each people, necessary
principles or conditions. Thus the legitimate monarchy and
liberty are the absolute conditions of our government because
they are the absolute needs of France. Separate liberty from
legitimacy and you go back to barbarism; separate legitimacy

---

[27] Quoted by Pouthas, *op. cit.,* p. 320, from "Philosophie Politique."

[28] For a definitive work on the Charter, see Pierre Simon, *L'Élaboration
de la Charte Constitutionnelle de 1814* (Paris, 1906), especially the critical,
annotated text of the Charter, pp. 121 ff.

from liberty and you bring back those horrible battles where both succumbed. . . . The Charter is nothing else than this indissoluble alliance of the legitimate power from whence it emanates with the national liberties which it recognizes and consecrates. . . . Although the Charter is written, and we have seen it written, it is not arbitrary . . . it has imposed itself by being true, by expressing faithfully the interests, manners, the state of the society it ought to rule.[29]

Although we will find, when we turn from political theory to political reality, that the sovereignty of reason was not to be established on earth quite this easily, Royer-Collard never abandoned his mystical view of the Charter. If he later conceded that the Charter's logic was "false at each line" because it embodied "contradictory principles," he always insisted that it would nevertheless endure because, with these principles, it truly reflected French society.[30] "La Charte est maintenant toute notre histoire."[31]

The Reform Whigs have sometimes been identified with the Austinian concept of sovereignty.[32] Taken at face value, some of Brougham's and Thomas Babington Macaulay's statements might seem to justify this. Brougham at one point declared: "In every state it appears . . . that there must be somewhere a Supreme and Sovereign power—an authority somewhere vested, and exercised in some specified manner, but in itself absolute."[33] And Macaulay dismissed the idea of independent parliaments within the Empire by observing,

---

[29] Barante, *op. cit.*, II, 16.   [30] *Ibid.*, p. 460.   [31] *Ibid.*, p. 233.

[32] For example, Crane Brinton, *English Political Thought in the 19th Century* (London: Ernest Benn, 1933), p. 39; and H. A. L. Fisher, *The Whig Historians* (London: Humphrey Milford, 1928), p. 32. Johnson, *op. cit.*, p. 41, seems to make the same error by contrasting Guizot's theory of sovereignty with the English reform movement's acceptance of Austin, thus missing the very real contrast between Benthamite and reform Whig views of sovereignty.

[33] *Political Philosophy* (London, 1846), I, 66.

"there cannot really be more than one supreme power in a society."[34]

To leave the Whig concept of sovereignty at this, however, is too simple. If Brougham and Macaulay seemed to start with Austin, the development of their ideas led in quite another direction and involved some fundamental quarrels with the whole Benthamite movement. Unlike either John Austin or Jeremy Bentham, the Whigs worshipped "checks and balances" and the "sacred principle of resistance." Again we are at the heart of the problem of reconciling the idea of sovereignty with a pluralized political system. While the Doctrinaires postulated philosophically the "sovereignty of reason" and then went on to the theory of the mixed state as the device for eliciting reason from society, the Whigs simply reversed the process. They started with a defense of a mixed state which had actually existed since 1688, and then in explaining how that state worked, they stumbled their way to something remarkably similar to the Doctrinaire concept. Behind this process was a view of "man" and of "reason" which was also similar to the Doctrinaires' and radically different from that of the Benthamites.

As with the French *juste milieu*, the object of the ideal Whig polity was "preventing one body in the government . . . from ruling uncontrolled."[35] To follow Brougham's argument, "the supreme power is lodged in more than one functionary or body." But not just any division of power will do. The division must involve "different kinds of power" and must guarantee the "separate and independent existence of different estates or authorities . . . each armed with some independent power of resistance to the others."[36] The "most perfect" mixed state "consists of a body representing each class,—the people by their own deputies, the men

---

[34] *History of England* (Boston: Houghton Mifflin, 1899), X, 53–54.
[35] Brougham, *Political Philosophy*, III, 158.   [36] *Ibid.*, pp. 146–47, 158.

of rank and wealth by the aristocratic chamber, and the executive departments of the state . . . by the sovereign."[37]

Obviously Austinian sovereignty was already in trouble. Having divided supreme power, Brougham first declared, "the sovereign or absolute will is that of all together."[38] Thirty pages later he conceded that in the mixed polity, "it is by no means easy to fix upon the owner of the supreme power."[39] The real subversion of Austin came, however, with the Whig reply to the Benthamite attack on the mixed state.

The Utilitarians rejected Whig "checks and balances" on two counts. First, since all individual pursuits of happiness would, by Bentham's philosophy, somehow tally up to the "greatest good for the greatest number," the only need was a single, popularly elected chamber. With that, an "identity of interest" would be assured between government and community. No complicated machinery was required to detect a "public interest" which would register itself automatically. "The community cannot have an interest opposite to its interest . . . this would be a contradiction in terms. . . . One community may intend the evil of another; never its own. This is an indubitable proposition."[40] In the Whig state, if the Crown and Lords represented "public interest," they were superfluous to the lower chamber. If they did not, they themselves were "sinister" interests.

Secondly, the Utilitarians claimed that the Whig ideal was, in fact, impossible. This argument was grounded in their view of human nature. To cite James Mill's judgment:

That one human being will desire to render the person and the property of another subservient to his pleasures, notwithstanding the pain or loss of pleasure which it may occasion to

---

[37] *Ibid.*, p. 160.   [38] *Ibid.*, I, 66.   [39] *Ibid.*, p. 91.

[40] James Mill, *Essay on Government* (New York: Liberal Arts Press, 1955), pp. 52, 67 ff.

that other individual, is the foundation of government.

There is no limit, therefore. . . . A man is never satisfied with a smaller degree if he can obtain a greater. . . . The demand . . . of power over the acts of other men is really boundless.[41]

What does this mean in terms of the mixed state? Quite simply that in a government of three branches each will necessarily try to aggrandize its own "wealth and power . . . as much as possible." The obvious means will be for any two to combine and destroy the third. "That such combination will take place appears to be as certain as anything that depends on human will." The mixed state of only two powers will meet a comparable fate. If the two powers are unequal, "it follows as a necessary consequence . . . that the stronger will take from the weaker till it engrosses the whole." That leaves only the possibility of two exactly equal powers. But, as a practical consideration, "the chances are as infinity to one" against such equality ever being established or preserved. In short, the entire Whig theory was "chimerical and absurd."[42]

The Whig answer to this attack must be kept in perspective. For as long as the Benthamites stuck to the practical world of common sense reform, the Whigs were often their allies and have been justly credited with helping popularize "utility" for English middle-class consumption. The practical influence of Bentham was clear in Brougham's various proposals for economic, educational, and legal reform. Macaulay on occasion even parrotted the "pleasure-pain" calculus: "As Christians surely we are bound to consider first, whether by excluding the Jews from all public trust, we give them pain; and, secondly, whether it be necessary to give them that pain in order to avert some evil."[43] Also, it was through Macau-

[41] *Ibid.*, pp. 56–57.   [42] *Ibid.*, pp. 62–66.
[43] *Op. cit.*, I, 116 (in House of Commons, April 17, 1833).

lay's legal code for India that Bentham became, in Halévy's phrase, the "posthumous legislator"[44] for England's largest possession.

But when the Benthamites turned to philosophizing about such things as the mixed state, they received little but contempt from the Whigs. The trouble was, as Brougham insisted, that the study of politics is a "practical, experimental science" whose "contingent" truths can never be susceptible to the kind of precise, abstract proof in which the Utilitarians delighted.[45] Macaulay brutally castigated James Mill as "an Aristotelian of the 15th century, born out of season," from whose *Essay on Government* "it would not appear that the author was aware that any governments actually existed among men."[46] Mill's deduction of a theory of government from "human nature" was "utterly impossible." The true sequence was precisely the opposite. "Our knowledge of human nature, instead of being prior . . . to our knowledge . . . of government, will be posterior to it."[47] We simply cannot talk about the real world of political experience as we talk of "lines and numbers."[48]

Turning to the real world, the Whigs disclaimed any idealistic picture of the mixed state as a perfect equipoise functioning without friction or resistance. But this was hardly to concede the basic Benthamite premise that "everyone is at all times sure to do whatever he is able to do."[49] "Human nature is not what Mr. Mill conceives it to be; . . . civilized men pursuing their own happiness in a social state, are not Yahoos fighting for carrion."[50] If that were true, said Broug-

---

[44] *The Growth of Philosophic Radicalism*, trans. Mary Morris (London: Faber and Faber, 1928), p. 510.   [45] *Political Philosophy*, 1, 2–3, 15–16.

[46] "Mill's Essay on Government," *Critical, Historical and Miscellaneous Essays* (New York: Sheldon, 1862), II, 8.

[47] "The Westminster Reviewer's Defence of Mill," *Essays*, II, 76–77.

[48] "Mill's Essay on Government," *Essays*, II, 18.

[49] Brougham, *Political Philosophy*, II, 9.

[50] Macaulay, "Mill's Essay on Government," *Essays*, II, 34.

ham, "the whole frame of civil society must be destroyed, and
all governments subverted."[51] Instead of the Benthamite
man, Brougham found a pervading "reasonableness" in human nature. The Whig explanation of the mixed state was
simply that one power would be "capable of limiting the
exercise of another," assuming that "none of the powers is in
itself absolute, *or would even if left to itself be carried to all
extremities.*" The "efficacy of the check" is "always . . . the
general reluctance of all parties to risk the consequences of
driving matters to extremities." And this "reluctance to bring
on collision will always operate, *however disproportioned the
forces.*" True, the various powers of government do not
always coincide, but usually they differ only "angularly,"
leaving the possibility of a "diagonal" result acceptable to all.
The mixed state works because of man's "universal disposition to avoid running risks."[52]

If Brougham himself here seemed to be talking "lines and
numbers," Macaulay put the Whig argument in somewhat
earthier terms. "Mr. Mill may say what he likes; but the
English Constitution is still alive." Its history of a constantly
shifting balance of power, back and forth among the Crown,
Lords, and Commons, should warn Mill that "in politics two
is not always the double of one." Mr. Mill "reminds us of the
Irishman who could not understand how one juryman could
possibly starve out eleven others."[53]

As for the Utilitarian counter that the formal powers of the
Constitution were only "semblances" masking rule by the
aristocracy, Macaulay declared that Mill was "still more in
the wrong" if he meant to discuss "power in a deeper and
philosophical sense. . . . For, if he had considered in what
the power of one human being over other human beings

---

[51] *Political Philosophy*, II, 9.   [52] *Ibid.*, pp. 6–12 (italics mine).
[53] "Mill's Essay on Government," *Essays*, II, 25, 27. See also Macaulay's
"Utilitarian Theory of Government," *Essays*, II, 98.

must ultimately consist, he would have perceived not only that there are mixed governments in the world, but that all the governments in the world . . . are mixed."[54] Why? Simply because the "fear of resistance" from his subjects limits, to a degree, even the most absolute ruler. "His power depends on their obedience; and . . . he can only enforce the unwilling obedience of some by the willing obedience of others." Granted Mill's view of the English Constitution for the sake of argument, the English people still have "in their hands a sufficient guarantee that in some points the aristocracy will conform to their wishes. . . . Therefore, the English Government is mixed."[55]

But the problem of obedience did more than answer Mill's objection to the mixed state. It also completed the subversion of Austinian sovereignty:

Constitutions are in politics what paper money is in commerce. . . . They are not power, but symbols of power, and will, in an emergency, prove altogether useless unless the power for which they stand be forthcoming. *The real power by which the community is governed is made up of all the means which all its members possess of giving pleasure or pain to each other.*[56]

Just as a state of barter suggests the real nature of money, the community of nations suggests the real nature of power:

There we find nothing analogous to a constitution: but do we not find a government? We do in fact find government in its purest, and simplest, and most intelligible form. . . . We see the principle of balance in constant operation . . . sometimes undisturbed . . . by encroachment for 20 or 30 years; and all this is produced . . . solely by the mutual hopes and fears of the various members.[57]

[54] *Ibid.*, p. 105.   [55] *Ibid.*, pp. 105–7.
[56] *Ibid.*, p. 109 (italics mine).   [57] *Ibid.*, pp. 109–10.

Now this statement should not be taken to imply that Macaulay was concerned with the relation between the internal and external implications of sovereignty—that is, between the problem of an institutional sovereign within a given nation and the problem of national sovereignty at the international level. Just as the Doctrinaires failed to explore the significance of the sovereignty of reason at that higher level, so the Whigs, preoccupied with the internal dynamics of government, never really developed the latent meaning which the working of the mixed state might have in terms of the outward sovereignty of the nation.[58]

What Macaulay's illustration from the community of nations in effect did was rather to shatter by analogy the Austinian idea of a single, determinate, institutional sovereign within government. Not only is the balance among the formal powers of government a continuing process of adjustment. More important, the "real governing power" is diffused in the complexity of the society underlying those powers. Finally, the very possibility of government is grounded in the supposed "reasonableness" of man's nature. If with this argument the Whigs were matching Mill in degree of sheer assumption about human nature, what they were substituting for his self-seeking, calculating "reason" was obviously very similar to the prudential "reason" which the Doctrinaires enthroned as sovereign. Just as with Royer-Collard and Guizot, Whig reason meant "compromise" and the "middle course." And just as the Doctrinaires often paired "reason" and "justice" in discussing sovereignty, Brougham added another "most material" influence against

---

[58] Brougham did write several essays on the balance of power in foreign affairs, but these dealt almost exclusively with the then existing *ad hoc* military, economic, and other interests of the major powers and did not come to terms with the problem of national sovereignty. See "Balance of Power"; "General Principles of Foreign Policy"; and "War Measures as Connected with the Balance of Power" in *Lord Brougham's Works* (Edinburgh, 1872), VIII, 1 ff., 79 ff., 161 ff.

usurpation in the mixed state: the general belief in society that the constitution represented "strict law and right."[59]

To continue the analogy, although the Whig theorists seemed to discover the sovereignty of reason in the process of explaining how the mixed state worked, they also, like the Doctrinaires, believed the converse: that that polity was the optimum device for eliciting reason from society. For the Whigs individual reason was *not,* as Mill insisted, "as plain as the road from Charing Cross to St. Paul's."[60] Nor was public reason any mathematical sum which could be registered in a single, popularly elected chamber. On the contrary, reason was elusive, multifarious, and fragmentized throughout all the various interests of society. Hence the need for a mixed government to express this multifariousness. Public reason also embraced, à la Guizot, past, present, and future. Brougham might vaguely define "general utility" as the test of an institution, but he also accepted "long establishment" as a presumption of utility.[61] Macaulay expressed the same notion when he complained that Mill thought "only of the greatest good of a single generation." Concede him all else, he still had to prove "that the interest of every generation is identical with the interest of all succeeding."[62] Until he did, the Whigs would continue to deny any magic equation between the "interest of the many" and the "general good." More than that, they would continue to stand by the mixed state!

Political Reality

The differing terms in which the Doctrinaires and Whigs cast essentially the same *juste milieu* concept of sovereignty

[59] *Political Philosophy,* II, 9–10.
[60] Mill to Francis Place, Dec. 6, 1817, quoted in Wallas, *op. cit.,* p. 91.
[61] *Political Philosophy,* I, 48.
[62] "Mill's Essay on Government," *Essays,* II, 37–38.

obviously reflect, to a degree, the differing political contexts in which they were operating. Confronted at the outset by the massive contours of the Ancien Regime and the Revolution, what else could the Doctrinaires do but first postulate out of the blue a theory of sovereignty undercutting the exclusive claims of these extremes and then eulogize France's new mixed state as the institutionalization of that theory? On the other hand, the Whigs, blessed with a mixed system that had survived some 150 years without calamity, could well afford to reach the sovereignty of reason by the more circuitous route of explaining why that system had and could continue to work.

But to note this apparent adaptation to environment is hardly to say that the two solutions were equally viable. For if one looks beyond the artistry of the Doctrinaire theory, he finds profound weaknesses from which the French *juste milieu* was never to escape. Even with their initial category, the Doctrinaires revealed the ideological initiative which their adversaries held. If they gutted the traditional meaning of sovereignty, the fact that they could not escape the category itself dramatized the facility of the Revolution and the Ancien Regime, preoccupied respectively with popular and monarchical sovereignty, to impose the terms of dispute. (The contrast with the Whigs' relatively infrequent use of the word "sovereignty" is interesting.)

As for the theory of the Charter, "liberty" and "legitimacy" were also ideas propounded initially not by the *juste milieu* itself, but by the Revolution and the Ancien Regime. Moreover, the Doctrinaires' declaration of these ideas was essentially negative. Liberty and legitimacy were consecrated by Royer-Collard not for their own intrinsic worth, but each as a necessary defense against the abuses of the other—"barbarism" and "horrible battles." If the sovereignty of reason may seem at first glance to transcend negativism, the failure to provide a positive, unambiguous definition of reason betrays this impression. Granted that no other ideological posture was possible for the men of the *juste milieu,* the posture remained defensive.

What is even more significant is the almost incredible unreality of the Doctrinaires' theory of sovereignty and the Charter. Here is surely a classic illustration of a point suggested earlier: the middling mind's tendency to exaggerate the power of sweet reasonableness in situations where the center may be relevant in the sense of being needed, but is at the same time egregiously unrealistic. For the real world in which the Doctrinaires were attempting to establish their *juste milieu* was hardly characterized by the kind of reason which they enthroned as sovereign. The "prudential" man who went through life shunning extremes was far more the exception than the rule in French Restoration politics, and to base a theory of sovereignty and government on his alleged omnipresence was hazardous indeed. The belief that the Charter would endure simply because it reflected French society is equally amazing. If society itself is rent by virtual civil war between its extremes, the constitution which reflects or tries to institutionalize that conflict cannot carry great promise of enduring. Guizot must have sensed this when he wrote, "The Charter itself has become their field of battle; it is within the treaty of peace that they search for weapons with which to reopen the war."[63] Yet, despite this flash of insight, he craved the same definitive settlement that the Charter symbolized for Royer-Collard and on another occasion, in eulogizing the document, observed, "La France est facile à gouverner."[64]

If the egregious unreality of this last remark need not be labored, the impact which political reality had on Doctrinaire theory and strategy is worth illustrating. Take, for ex-

[63] "Du Gouvernement Représentatif en France, en 1816," *Mélanges Politiques et Historiques* (Paris, 1869), I, 9.
[64] *Ibid.,* p. 80.

ample, the Doctrinaires' response to the most important problem of the mixed state which the Charter had left unresolved. That was the question whether the King was obligated to select his ministers from the parliamentary majority. It was clear in the Charter that the power of appointing individual ministers did rest with the King and also that ministers could be held *criminally* responsible through impeachment in parliament in cases of treason or peculation. But the document was silent on whether the ministers were also to be *politically* responsible to parliament in the sense that the continued life of a cabinet depended upon majority support.

After the elections of August 1815 had returned the notorious Chambre Introuvable ("more royalist than the King himself"), Guizot and Royer-Collard argued strongly against such political responsibility to the Chamber. Supporting the moderate Richelieu ministry against the enormous Ultra majority, Royer-Collard theorized that the approval of legislation initiated by the King and ministry was always to be "presumed." In the case of financial legislation, approval was "indispensable." Underlying that argument was Royer-Collard's conviction, at this date, that the individual deputy should remain independent of either party or majority discipline. He declared, "the day that the government is at the discretion of the majority of the Chamber . . . that day, all is finished not only with the Charter, but with our royalty. . . . That day we are a republic."[65] Although Guizot, unlike Royer-Collard, always valued the strength which a parliamentary majority could give a ministry, he too insisted at the time that the life of a ministry should not depend on that majority.[66] Conversely, the Ultras were equally obvious in attempting to capitalize their parliamentary strength by embracing the idea of ministerial responsibility to the

[65] Barante, *op. cit.,* I, 216–17.
[66] "Du Gouvernement Représentatif," *Mélanges,* I, 44–46.

Chamber. Baron de Vitrolles even matched Benjamin Constant by insisting that parliamentary government depended on the division of the Chamber into two distinct, fixed parties. Vicomte de Chateaubriand, Comte de Villèle, Baron de Frénilly, and a variety of others joined in this call for parliamentary practice on the English model as a convenient device for securing Ultra dominance.[67]

But as so often happened in Restoration France, strategic conveniences soon changed and brought an exact reversal of the Ultra and Doctrinaire theories of ministerial responsibility. From 1816 to 1820 elections reduced the Ultras to a minority in the Chamber and suggested to the Doctrinaires that Ultra supremacy there was by no means inevitable. Although the assassination of the Duc de Berri and elections in 1820 under a narrowed franchise restored declining Ultra strength, the second and rightist Richelieu ministry did not command a disciplined majority. The Doctrinaires now opposed Richelieu's new policies of repression with exactly the opposite of the argument that they had made earlier. Royer-Collard now accused the premier, "You no longer have a majority, I mean a true majority. . . . The false majorities which succeed one another are basically only minorities, accidentally enlarged by different or even opposed opinions." He even described it as a "supreme prerogative of the Chamber" to refuse appropriations to a minister.[68] Guizot joined in this attack. Now he chose to emphasize that any denial to the Chamber of a decisive influence in the formation of the ministry was a denial of representative government.[69] This

---

[67] Baron de Vitrolles, *Du Ministère dans le Gouvernement Représentatif* (Paris, 1815), pp. 69 ff. Chateaubriand's *La Monarchie selon la Charte* (Paris, 1816) was also an important document in this Ultra move. See discussion in J. Barthélemy, *Introduction du Régime Parlementaire en France sous Louis XVIII et Charles X* (Paris, 1904), pp. 168–81; and Rémond, *op. cit.*, pp. 24–25.

[68] Barante, *op. cit.*, II, 9, 47, 156.

[69] *Du Gouvernement de la France depuis la Restauration*, p. 284.

same theme continued to recur in Doctrinaire dialectics during the latter part of the Villèle ministry and was also a major premise in the opposition to Charles X's choice of Polignac as premier over and against a strongly liberal Chamber.

This zigzag maneuver on an important operative detail of the mixed state highlights both the positional and the unreal dimensions of Doctrinaire theory. As Guizot was to observe in later years after another bit of fancy footwork, "I remain, I am always with the *juste milieu.*"[70] One may be tempted, à la Michel and Soltau, to dismiss such a remark as opportunism compounded by cynicism. But in the political context of the day, this was not an opportunism simply to gain personal power or office or to win support wherever it might be available. One can argue instead that the Doctrinaires were pursuing the only plausible strategy for defending a narrow center besieged on two fronts. At the same time, without being inconsistent, one can also conclude that the position itself and the hope of enthroning reason on earth deserve far more the description of "dream" than of "opportunism."

For on the Royalist front the significant fact in French politics—especially in contrast with English—was the control which extremism acquired over the bulk of the right in the late 1820s. Without that control Charles would probably not have dared the selection of Polignac. Nor would he have dared the July ordinances which brought the Revolution: dissolution of the newly elected liberal parliament, drastic restriction of the franchise, and a virtual blackout of press rights. On the opposite flank the extreme left had only marginal parliamentary strength during the Restoration. But the left did possess latent extra-parliamentary resources, of which the barricades of July 1830 were impressive evidence, and it wielded always a peculiar facility for striking fear in the

[70] *Histoire Parlementaire,* III, 184.

hearts of the men of the center. In turn, the presence of the Revolution on the left and the memory of the Terror drastically restricted the ground on which the Doctrinaires felt safe in combating the right. To draw support from the left against the right seemed always to risk the victory of the Revolution. For example, in 1819, just as the Doctrinaires were gaining on the right, they were confronted with fire on their other flank: the election of twenty-nine members of the left, led by General Maximilien-Sébastien Foy and the former regicide Henri Grégoire. Guizot worriedly called this "une insulte grave" to the *juste milieu,* and a year later, in opposing the second Richelieu ministry, Royer-Collard took special care to avoid being "in rapport with the liberal revolutionaries."[71]

Significantly enough, Grégoire's election at Grenoble was made possible only by a bloc vote of Ultra electors. As Chateaubriand declared, "It is necessary to make the king swallow some Jacobins, in order to make him surrender the ministers whom he has in his stomach."[72] This was neither the first nor the last *ad hoc* alliance between the extremes, and the tragedy of such Ultra traffic with the left was that it was never anything more than a wrecking operation against the center. Although Villèle made a curious reference on one occasion to George Canning's "Liberal Toryism,"[73] the Ultras failed to develop any similarly constructive, integrative movement.

Against this background it should be no wonder that the Doctrinaires failed to develop during the Restoration either an effective political party or a positive legislative program. Granted that the first failure involved a certain fondness for

[71] Guizot, *Du Gouvernement de la France depuis la Restauration,* p. 80; Barante, *op. cit.,* II, 63.

[72] Quoted in Thureau-Dangin, *Le Parti Libéral sous la Restauration* (Paris, 1876), p. 98.

[73] Comte de Villèle, *Mémoires et Correspondence* (Paris, 1887–90), II, 77. See also Barthélemy, *op. cit.,* p. 176.

independence, it also clearly reflected the narrowness of the ground on which they stood and their compulsive fear of the left. Moreover, these factors, and especially the latter, presaged the fatal mistake of Guizot's late July Regime in not establishing a working alliance with the liberal dynastic opposition immediately to its left. The Doctrinaire mind never ceased to see the specter of the Revolution behind even its moderate critics. The result, as Plamenatz has put it, was a "chain of friendship" on the left, beginning *outside* the *juste milieu* and stretching from Guizot's parliamentary opposition through "respectable" Republicans to Jacobins and Socialists.[74] Although the chain was often loose or broken, it held the potential, given the right crisis, of isolating the July Regime from all but Guizot's narrowly based parliamentary majority.

As for the second failure, the preoccupation of the Revolution and the Ancien Regime with organic change meant that the great disputes of the Restoration were largely over issues like ministerial responsibility, electoral laws, and press rights. The Doctrinaire response to these issues revealed much besides the strong positional strain of *juste milieu* thought. Assuming that their ideology did include some inherent ideals as well, the fact that the Doctrinaires were constantly involved in struggle over such basic constitutional issues precluded them from ever translating their ideals into the kind of practical, positive legislative program which one finds Radicals, Whigs, and Canningites alike developing in England. A viable legislative program presupposes a viable parliamentary system, and the latter was still in doubt.

Thus the genesis of France's 1830 hardly suggested that "reason" was sovereign in the world of politics which the Doctrinaires confronted. Preaching the power of reasona-

---

[74] *Op. cit.,* pp. 58 ff.

bleness might convince the Doctrinaires themselves that middlingness was a realistic cause, but that was hardly enough.
In a sense René Rémond is misleading when he observes,
"With the July Regime, it is in effect a school of thought
which comes to power, that of the Doctrinaires."[75] For it is
equally important to remember that the July Days also gave
the new regime the unfortunate parentage of revolution,
dramatized the still embattled position of the center, and
exposed the unreality of that initial *juste milieu* premise, the
sovereignty of reason. It was the Ultras who forced the Revolution, the Republicans who raised the barricades in Paris,
and only a handful of quick-witted moderates who saved the
day for constitutional monarchy. Little wonder that Royer-
Collard declared, "I am among the conquerors, but the victory is sad indeed."[76]

When one crosses the Channel he begins to see the sense of
the suggestion that the Doctrinaires, despite Royer-Collard's
moment of truth in 1830, were tacitly mistaking France for
England in propounding the sovereignty of reason. In
England the Whig faith in the "prudent man" who instinctively avoids pushing matters to "collision" rested on fairly
solid political reality. The problem in England is not to
square the Whigs' theory of sovereignty with the political
context in which they found themselves, but rather with their
insistence on a direct analogy between English and French
politics. In contrast with France, the breadth and stability of
the center are what impress one about English politics. If
there were "extremes," there was not a "chasm" between
them. To use Plamenatz' phrase again and switch metaphors,
there were "chains of friendship" on both the English left
and right, but significantly both chains began *within* the
juste milieu and stopped short of extremism.

[75] *Op. cit.*, p. 81.   [76] Barante, *op. cit.*, II, 446.

In addition to the Watsons, Hunts, and Thistlewoods who led the disorders after Waterloo, the English left also included a wide sector of moderate Radicals who might not waste any love on Whiggism, but who at the same time despised the republican-socialist illusions of the extremists. Without the compulsive fear of the left which the Terror had indelibly imprinted on the Doctrinaire mind, the Whigs found these Radicals fairly comfortable *ad hoc* allies — surely far more comfortable than the Republicans of the July Days had been for the men of the French *juste milieu*.

An example par excellence of this moderate breed was Francis Place, the celebrated "Radical Tailor of Charing Cross." Although Place delighted on occasion in calling the Whigs "dirty," "palsied," and "gabbling," he found himself, like the Whigs, fighting "war on two fronts" during the Reform Bill era.[77] Directing propaganda all over England, Place was as prodigious in his efforts against Ultra Radical as he was against Tory opposition to the Whig Bill. Perhaps he is best remembered for his ingenious plan for a mass run on banks in case Wellington replaced Grey in May 1832 ("To Stop the Duke, Go for Gold"). Yet the National Political Union, with which he expected to implement the plan, had originally been organized by Place as a counter-movement to the Ultra Radical National Union of the Working Classes, led by James Watson and Henry Hetherington, whose ideas had been inspired by the socialism of Robert Owen and Thomas Hodgskin. These men drew Place's condemnation as "reckless rascals. . . . Some were perfectly atrocious."[78] In good Whig parlance he described the difference between his own organization and the National Union: "the first desired the Reform Bill to prevent revolution, the

[77] Wallas, *op. cit.,* pp. 123, 179, 241, 261.
[78] *Ibid.,* p. 273. See also M. Beer, *British Socialism* (London: Allen & Unwin, 1953), I, 299 ff.

last desired its destruction as the means of producing revolution."[79] Fortunately for the Whigs, Place proved the superior tactician and solidified the London working classes around the cause of moderate reform.

Thomas Attwood of Birmingham was another important point of contact between Whiggism and Radicalism. During the Reform struggle Attwood enthusiastically placed his famous Birmingham Union, originally organized as a vehicle for his currency scheme, in the service of the Whig cause. In doing so he found himself, like Place, fighting on two fronts, for the National Union was also established in Birmingham as an enemy of Whig moderation.

If Royer-Collard and Guizot feared anyone and everyone to their left, not so the Whigs. They encouraged rather than turned their backs on this moderate Radical assistance. Lord Melbourne, then Home Secretary and hardly an habitué of working-class circles, paid Place the compliment of asking him to use his influence to end sporadic outbreaks of violence in the agricultural districts.[80] In recognition of Attwood's services, Grey successfully resisted the King's demand for forcible repression of all organizations like the Birmingham Union. More than that, in the face of charges that he was a "traitor to his class," he also corresponded personally with Attwood concerning the terms of the Reform Bill.[81]

The deeper meaning of this moderate Radical-Whig collaboration was not just that the Bill passed, but that the Whigs were never to be so completely isolated from the left as were the Doctrinaires in France. In a moment of exultation, the *Westminster Review* even declared, "the estrange-

---

[79] Wallas, *op. cit.*, p. 290.

[80] G. M. Trevelyan, *Lord Grey of the Reform Bill* (London: Longmans, 1929), p. 286.

[81] *Ibid.*, p. 349; Butler, *op. cit.*, p. 249. For other instances of contact between Whig and Radical leaders, see Hamburger, *op. cit.*, pp. 56 ff. and 267 ff.

ment which had long been growing between the Whigs and the community has . . . been removed. . . . The Whigs are now as they were in 1688."[82] Although the *Review,* Place, and Attwood were to have their quarrels with the Whigs in later years, the "chain of friendship" on the left was clearly not the menace to the *juste milieu* that it was in France. It was rather a potential source of strength, for given a crisis—such as the more virulent stages of Chartism—the moderate Radicals invariably aligned with the *juste milieu,* not extremism. It was thus the far left, not the *juste milieu,* which stood in danger of isolation. Finally, in terms of political theory, this moderate breed of Radicalism obviously gave the Whig concept of "reasonableness" an important substance of reality.

Even more reality is added when one looks to the Whigs' other flank. For "prudent" men were not uncommon in Tory, as well as Whig and Radical ranks. If in France extremists like Polignac succeeded in dominating the right during the late Restoration, in England it is fair to say that the moderate Tories emerged with the balance of power within their party. Perhaps the most significant Tory turn toward liberalism came in 1822 under the Earl of Liverpool with the accession of William Huskisson to the Board of Trade, Robert Peel to the Home Office, and George Canning to the Foreign Office. Despite the resistance of these men to any large extension of the franchise, the impressive economic, penal, and other reforms which they carried won wide approval in both Radical and Whig circles. The *Morning Chronicle,* expressing the views of Mill and Ricardo, eulogized Huskisson for his tariff reductions. Thomas Tooke, free trade economist, declared that its internal policies put the Liverpool cabinet in advance not only of the public, but of the mercantile community itself.[83] Brougham was

[82] XIV (April 1831), 455.
[83] Leslie Stephen, *The English Utilitarians* (London, 1900), II, 52, 54.

equally extravagant in his praise, and his fellow Whig, Robert Heron, even predicted that if Tory liberalism continued, "the opposition will dwindle into nothing."[84]

Brougham, however, saw another alternative for the Whig opposition. Ever since 1820 he had been attempting to maneuver a coalition of Whigs and liberal Tories in order "to disunite and finally break up the Tory party."[85] Brougham's idea was to Whigize the Canningites and let the ultra Tories be the ones to "dwindle into nothing." When Canning succeeded as Prime Minister in 1827, Brougham's strategy got its trial in a coalition which gave cabinet rank to three Whigs—George Tierney, the Marquis of Lansdowne, and the Earl of Carlisle. Macaulay now exulted that the Whigs and Canningites were "perfectly agreed" in foreign and commercial policy and could be distinguished only by "badges."[86] Although the coalition was cut short within the year by Canning's death, the schism within the Tory party between the Wellingtonian old guard and the liberals widened. Huskisson, for example, resigned from the Wellington cabinet of 1828 within only six months and was followed by Lord Palmerston, Charles Grant, and William Lamb, the future Lord Melbourne.

Ironically, having just lost most of the Canningites, Wellington and Peel then made the "great surrender" of granting Catholic Emancipation in 1829. If this somewhat redeemed the Duke in Whig eyes, it completed the splintering of the Tory party by alienating men like the Duke of Cumberland and Lord Eldon who stood to the right of even Wellington. First isolated in his own party and then shaken by the general elections of 1830, Wellington next explored the possibility of a new, broad coalition which would include both

[84] S. Maccoby, *English Radicalism, 1786–1832* (London: Allen & Unwin, 1953), p. 390.

[85] Brougham, *Life and Times*, II, 331–32, 364; A. Aspinall, *Lord Brougham and the Whig Party* (Manchester University Press, 1927), pp. 100, 112, 116, 128–37.   [86] "The Present Administration," *Essays*, VI, 411, 413.

Whigs and Canningites. Although this very attempt was a reflection of the underlying spirit of compromise in English politics, it was unsuccessful. At last, in November 1830, the Whigs and Canningites voted together against the cabinet on the civil list, forcing Wellington's resignation and setting the stage for the reform ministry of Grey.

Against this background the Whig victory in 1832 was clearly to be less precarious than the Doctrinaires' in 1830. If Place and Attwood were safer allies than the Doctrinaires had on the July barricades, the English right was hardly the equivalent of the French. It was not simply that the right included the Canningites, whose economic views enabled them to traffic constructively across the wide middle ground of British politics. In the end even Wellington proved to be no Polignac. The Duke is reported to have declared once, "It was always Napoleon's object to win a great battle; my object, on the contrary, was always to avoid to fight a great battle."[87] However he might square this strategy with Waterloo, Wellington followed it to the letter in 1829 with Catholic Emancipation and again in May 1832 when he bowed out as a possible prime minister rather than fight a great battle with a tailor from Charing Cross Road who, in his own way, was fully as able a campaigner as Napoleon. What better illustration of the "prudence" and "reasonableness" with which the Whigs explained the mixed state? As Trollope was to put it in later years, "No reform, no innovation—experience almost justifies us in saying no revolution—stinks so foully in the nostrils of an English Tory politician as to be absolutely irreconcilable to him."[88] The political reality which underlay Trollope's judgment meant that 1832 could be a "reform," rather than a "revolution," and that the English *juste milieu* held some promise of being a vital center.

[87] Quoted by Michael Oakeshott, *Political Education* (Cambridge: Bowes & Bowes, 1951), title page.

[88] *The Bertrams* (London: Bodley Head, 1905), p. 281.

The Puzzle: Bristol and Lyons

The problem remains, however, to square the reality of the Whigs' theory of sovereignty with the unreality of their frequent insistence on a direct analogy between their position in English politics and that of the Doctrinaires in France. One interesting insight into the puzzle may be implicit in the argument recently advanced by Joseph Hamburger that the moderate Radicals, although *ad hoc* allies of the Whigs, deliberately exaggerated to the Whigs the true danger of imminent revolution in the country during the Reform Bill struggle. Hamburger documents that strategy effectively with admissions by Mill, Place, and others—largely in letters to each other—that they were indeed misrepresenting matters not only in the press but in reports to Whig ministers. The purpose of the strategy was to maintain continued pressure on the Whigs to pass the Bill as a concession which would smother popular discontent. Although Hamburger misses the Whig identification of English with French politics, the Radical exaggeration of discontent would surely tend to reenforce in Whig minds the relevance of the analogy. However, that influence alone hardly seems an adequate explanation of the English-French identification. The Whigs themselves had held and continued to hold their unreal view of English politics for a good many years before and after the 1830–32 period of Millite strategy. Indeed, Hamburger himself concedes that even without the prompting of Radical misinformation, the Whigs often expressed the same fears which the Radicals were trying to foster. At the same time, he does not attribute to those expressions the conscious strategy of deceit of which the Radicals were culpable.[89]

The alternative inference which I would offer is that the

[89] *Op. cit., passim,* and especially pp. 60 ff., 125 ff., 266 ff.

Whigs unwittingly held unreal fears and unwittingly believed Radical exaggerations for quite another reason: those
fears and exaggerations seemed to confirm so precisely in the
Whigs' own minds their image of themselves as a middling
party whose *raison d'être* was the prudential compromise of
formidable political extremes. And interestingly enough that
inference takes us back once again to the subtle trap to which
the middling mind seems so susceptible. That, as I have
suggested, is the trap of attempting to be both realistic and
relevant at the same time—of emphasizing, on the one hand,
the universal power of reasonableness, while conjuring up,
on the other hand, the specter of dangerous extremes to
provide some *raison d'être* for the center. The Doctrinaires'
concept of sovereignty could well be considered a kind of
compensation for the unreality of their position. In turn,
perhaps the Whigs' exaggeration of left and right and their
credulous response to Radical reports were an unwitting
attempt to make their preoccupation with avoiding extremes
rather more relevant than it really was. One can surely say
this without implying that middlingness was irrelevant in
early nineteenth-century England. The Whig error, innocent
or not, was instead one of degree.

To be a bit less speculative, even though England had itself
escaped the Great Revolution, that cataclysm had occurred
close enough to home to make France a continuing point of
reference for Englishmen of all parties well into the
nineteenth century. One must also remember that Trollope's
faith in the reconcilability of English politics reflected the
hindsight of the 1850s. In the rush of events of the earlier
decades, it was hardly so easy for *anyone*—right, left, or
center—to be certain that Wellington would not prove a
Polignac or that Place would faithfully resist republican-
socialist illusions. And regardless of any exaggeration of popular discontent, England did experience enough actual outbreaks of violence in the first half of the century so that the

French analogy must often have seemed plausible. One of these, the Bristol riots of 1831, often compared to the Lyons silk-workers' insurrection of the same year, deserves more than passing mention. For on the surface the events at Bristol make the temptation to identify England with France quite understandable, while at the same time the underlying contrast between Bristol and Lyons confirms that the identification was indeed a mistake.

Although the Bristol riots occurred against a background of economic distress, they were triggered by the Lords' rejection of the Whigs' second reform proposal, a notable lapse in the sovereignty of reason, and the visit of Bristol's Tory Recorder, Sir Charles Wetherell, for the annual jail delivery. Over a three-day period a mob, shouting "King and Reform," managed to burn, among other buildings, the mansion house, the bishop's palace, the customs house, the toll house, and the jail—surely a sufficient amount of arson to frighten even the most cool-headed. However, two other aspects of the riots are really more significant than their magnitude. First, the violence at Bristol was sudden, unplanned, and unorganized. This gave the riots that same character which most English outbreaks of the period, including those right after Waterloo, had in contrast with French disorders. Although the Hammonds[90] and others of their generation liked to read coherent class motivation into such violence and saw the government's response as a systematic, Czarist-like conspiracy to suppress freedom, more recent historical judgment has stressed confusion and absence of purpose as the hallmark of these outbreaks. As R. J. White observes in his recent study, "The disease from which England was suffering was rather one of *dis*organization

[90] For example, "Probably no English Government has ever been quite so near, in spirit and license, to the atmosphere that we used to associate with the Tsar's government of Russia as the Government that ruled England for the first few years of the peace" (J. L. and Barbara Hammond, *The Skilled Labourer* [London: Longmans, 1919], p. 371).

than of diabolical possession."[91] In contrast with both the forces of revolution and repression in France, this is surely convincing. For example, there was no organizational network comparable to the French *Charbonnerie* behind the English disorders, and the motley array of "Bow Street runners" in London and amateur constables in the country who attempted to keep the peace were scarcely the equivalent of the centralized police apparatus which Paris had available. Even when the military was called into action, the difference was still apparent. If a single officer and company of men were dispatched to handle the riots at Bristol, the job of putting down the insurrection at Lyons was entrusted to an army of 40,000 men under the personal command of the heir to the throne and the minister of war.[92]

Secondly, the Bristol riots could not be blamed exclusively on the lower classes or what is usually meant by the "mob." Contemporary accounts referred significantly to the number of "respectable citizens" and "tradesmen" who, particularly on the first day, either led, took part in, or tacitly approved of the outburst.[93] While later prosecuting one Patrick Kearney as a leader, the attorney general noted that he was "a man possessed of some little property" and complained:

The effect of such a man going among a mob, must be most mischievous, because it tends to hold out encouragement to

---

[91] *Waterloo to Peterloo* (London: Heinemann, 1957), p. 176. See also Hamburger, *op. cit.*, pp. 112–202; and Donald Read, *Peterloo* (Manchester University Press, 1958), *passim* and especially p. 207, at which he declares, "Any parallels between government policy in England and on the Continent after 1815 are false ones: there can be no smooth historical generalizations about a European 'Age of Repression' after Waterloo."

[92] Halévy, *History of the English People*, III, 51.

[93] Although most general histories of the period deal too cursorily with the Bristol riots to make this point, it is clear in both the pro- and anti-reform pamphlet accounts of the day. For example, John Eagles (Tory), *The Bristol Riots* (Bristol, 1832), pp. 62, 72, 81; and W. H. Somerton (Radical), *Narrative of the Bristol Riots* (Bristol, n.d., *circa* 1832), pp. 14, 85. See also Hamburger, *op. cit.*, pp. 174 ff.

the most depraved portion of society, by lending to it the countenance of those who are somewhat higher in the scale of society than themselves.[94]

It may well be that this "respectable" element was one of a number of factors which led the commander of the troops at Bristol to temporize with the gathering mob until it was too late to control matters. If that is speculative, all accounts of the riots do agree that had the troops taken immediate, forceful action, the outburst would have been only a minor incident.

At Lyons, in contrast, the insurrection clearly had a solid working-class base. Moreover, the assumption of authority in the city by the workers had been preceded by carefully defined demands for higher wages, and was executed with remarkable discipline and organization. Violence was kept to a necessary minimum and looting by the insurgents was unknown. It was orderliness, not confusion, which was impressive. No one has ever quarreled with Louis Blanc's assertion that life and property (including the government mint and homes of manufacturers) were "never better guarded" than during the Lyons rising.[95]

Yet only at first glance does the violence of Bristol seem a more frightening manifestation of revolution than Lyons. If Soult's army was perhaps an excessive show of force, Paris was nevertheless right in sensing that the very orderliness of the Lyons rising reflected class consciousness and deep social discontent among the workers—discontent which the bourgeois regime of 1830 had not and could not satisfy. Bristol, however, for all its arson, still left hope. For one thing, it was

[94] Eagles, *op. cit.,* p. 247; and Somerton, *op. cit.,* p. 21. Both include accounts of the subsequent trials.

[95] *History of Ten Years, 1830–1840* (London, 1844), I, 541; Asa Briggs, "Social Structure and Politics in Birmingham and Lyons," *British Journal of Sociology,* I (March 1950), 77; M. D. R. Leys, *Between Two Empires* (London: Longmans, 1955), pp. 197–200.

hardly necessary to stand helpless while "respectable" tradesmen ran amuck with the mob. Place proved in London and
Attwood in Birmingham that, given the right organization,
this kind of middle-class reform agitation could be disciplined and turned *against* the mob.[96] For another thing, even
where such a framework was lacking, as it obviously was at
Bristol, there remained the possibility that a generous grant
of the franchise to the middle classes could end the occasional
incongruous alliance of respectability with rabble and shatter
the disorganized forces of revolution. That solution was precisely what the Whigs proposed with the Great Reform Bill.
The Lyons-Bristol contrast is thus an appropriate prelude to a
consideration of the Whig and Doctrinaire theory of middle-
class representation.

[96] Briggs, *op. cit.*, pp. 76–78, makes this point in contrasting Lyons and
Birmingham. See also his "Background of the Parliamentary Reform Move-
ment in Three English Cities (1830–32)," *Cambridge Historical Journal*,
X, No. 3 (1952), 293 ff.

Chapter Three

REPRESENTATION AND

THE MIDDLE CLASS

The Theory

THE Doctrinaires' theory of representation and apotheosis of the middle class, the ideas for which they are most often remembered, can be considered an elaboration of their concept of sovereignty. The Doctrinaires viewed human reason as not only fallible, but also unequally fragmentized throughout society. Individual will could not be its credential. For Royer-Collard, societies could not rightly be considered mere "numerical sums of individuals and wills." The true stuff of society consisted of "rights and interests in place of individuals and wills." In turn, the recurring concept of "interest," prefaced by such adjectives as "veritable" and "legitimate," provided the "sanction of representative government." It was not a certain total of wills which the elective chamber ought to represent, but rather those "interests" which, in Doctrinaire theory, embodied earthly reason.[1] Guizot's favorite formulation of this theme was to quote Pascal: "Plurality which does not reduce itself to unity, is confusion. Unity which is not the result of plurality, is tyranny." The plurality, for Guizot, was the certain number of "just ideas . . . unequally diffused" among men. The unity was the work of representation, "a natural process by which public reason . . . may be extracted from the bosom of society."[2] In the end, Royer-Collard declared, true representative government not only represents all the legitimate

[1] Barante, *op. cit.,* II, 463–64. See also I, 229; II, 36; and Guizot, "Élections," *Discours Académiques,* p. 412.
[2] *History of Representative Government,* pp. 62, 347–48.

interests of society, "but does so more faithfully than society itself would be able to do."[3]

Some of the specifics by which this happy result was to be reached reveal that same positional quality which we have already seen in the *juste milieu* switch on ministerial responsibility. In the early Restoration, once more against the background of the Chambre Introuvable, the Doctrinaires attempted to insulate the deputies from both the nation and electorate. Royer-Collard even insisted that constitutionally there was no link between electorate and Chamber. "The Charter being the sole title of its existence . . . it is the Charter which constitutes the Chamber, and not election."[4] The electors voted not by "right," but as "functionaries" created by the Charter's 300 franc provision.[5] Conversely the Ultras, attempting to exploit their early electoral success against a king who was proving too moderate, declared that the deputies of the Chamber must be regarded as "organs of national opinion."[6] Villèle's confidence in the royalism of "national opinion" was at one point so great that he even proposed to enlarge the electorate enormously by lowering the property qualification to a mere 50 franc tax rate.[7]

After the elections from 1816 to 1820 had reflected a trend toward liberalism in the country, the Doctrinaires and Ultras reversed positions. If the Ultras soon lost interest in electoral reform, the Doctrinaires tried to consolidate the moderates' position by conceding a link between the Chamber and nation. Contradicting virtually word for word what he had said earlier, Royer-Collard announced, "Whence comes the force of the elective Chamber? *From election, its name so pro-*

---

[3] Barante, *op. cit.,* II, 36.

[4] *Ibid.,* I, 228–29. In making a case against representation of will, Royer-Collard even took a leaf from Rousseau by arguing, "wills . . . are either themselves or they are not" (II, 464).   [5] *Ibid.,* I, 271.

[6] Barthélemy, *op. cit.,* p. 176; Vitrolles, *op. cit.,* pp. 29–30.

[7] Achille de Vaulabelle, *Histoire des Deux Restaurations* (Paris, 1847), IV, 53.

claims."[8] The reign of Charles X brought the Doctrinaires to an even more liberal view of the electorate. With the Ultras entrenched in the Villèle-Martignac-Polignac ministries, Royer-Collard opposed a scheme to restrict the franchise because it would eliminate "that portion of the electors, who, finding themselves nearest the working classes, put the elective Chamber in rapport and harmony with the masses."[9] Then in 1830 the famous "address of the 221," setting the stage for the July Revolution, formally insisted on that link between nation and government so carefully avoided in 1815–16. The Charter now consecrated, "as a right, the intervention of the country in the deliberation of public interests."[10]

The insistence on a property qualification for the franchise was one aspect of the Doctrinaire theory of representation which escaped this kind of positionally determined compromise. This should not surprise, since the idea of a property qualification involved, as we will see, the Doctrinaires' view of the middle class and thus, by the Huntington typology, could be presumed to be an inherent, rather than positional, category. Guizot developed the property theme with a virtual paraphrase of Aristotelian proportional equality. There are "rights that man possesses by the fact that he is man." Among these are "liberty of conscience and most rights that we call civil." Such rights are "equal and the same for all." However, there are also "unequal rights which distribute themselves according to the natural inequalities it pleases Providence to establish among men." The right of political participation is of the second class: "it is subordinate to the capacity of individuals." Capacity, in turn, "is nothing less than the faculty of acting in accordance with reason."[11] If

[8] Barante, *op. cit.,* II, 217 (italics mine).
[9] *Ibid.,* p. 282.   [10] *Ibid.,* p. 420.
[11] Guizot, *Du Gouvernement de la France depuis la Restauration,* p_r. xxxvi–xxxviii; *History of Representative Government,* p. 396.

will is not the credential of "capacity," what is? The answer
of Guizot and Royer-Collard was property. "A certain degree
of personal wealth" serves to establish "the presumption of
political judgment." The rationale was not that the more
property a man has the wiser he is, but rather that all those
who attain a given level of wealth are "equally capable."[12]
For "intelligence, in all careers . . . finds its place and
achieves fortune."[13]

Finally, those who attain this magic plane above the passions of the multitude are able to represent perfectly all the
"legitimate interests" of society. They compose an order
"which possesses in itself all those interests and not a single
contrary interest . . . and represents them perfectly, since it
cannot injure any of them without injuring itself."[14] This,
then, was Royer-Collard's "belle théorie de Platon." Guizot
spoke of the concept of political capacity as "perhaps the most
beautiful, the most useful conquest" of the Restoration, and
proclaimed that never before in history had such "a similarity
of interests" accompanied such "a diversity of professions and
inequality of conditions" as in the French Chamber of Deputies.[15]

At first glance the Burkean or "Old Whig"[16] overtones of
the Doctrinaire theory of representation seem impressive. As
I have already suggested, the French *juste milieu* theorists
had a view of "reason" and "social contract" quite similar to
Burke's. Both the Doctrinaires and Burke rejected an atom-
istic image of society and individual will as the basis of
representation in favor of the great "interests" which were
the true stuff of society. Both posited a deliberative assembly
of superior men, independent of electoral mandate, who

[12] Barante, *op. cit.,* I, 276; II, 21–22.
[13] Guizot, *Histoire Parlementaire,* III, 558.
[14] Barante, *op. cit.,* II, 464.   [15] *Histoire Parlementaire,* III, 556.
[16] Professor Samuel Beer's phrase. See his "Representation of Interests in
British Government," *American Political Science Review,* LI (Sept. 1957),
613 ff.

could not only represent those interests better than society itself, but who could also transcend them in what Burke called the "general reason of the whole." Just as Guizot lauded the representation of the French Chamber, Sir Robert Inglis described the pre-1832 House of Commons as "the most complete representation of the interests of the people which was ever assembled in any age or country."[17]

Interestingly enough, the *Edinburgh Review* in 1820 referred explicitly to the Doctrinaires' notion of "classing together similar interests," and declared, "we incline decidedly to their theory."[18] At this date the Whigs favored moderate parliamentary reform, but still defended the Old Whig or Burkean theory as the framework within which it should be made. If they quarreled with the Tory claim that the existing House of Commons excluded no important interests, they accepted the concept of interest representation and sensed the Old Whig overtones of Doctrinaire thought.

There are, however, some important discrepancies in the analogy just suggested. The development of the Doctrinaire theory of representation also involved elements of the "Old Tory" idea of royal initiative, which in England had preceded the Burkean theory, and of the "middle class mystique," which succeeded the Old Whig stage.[19] The men of the French *juste milieu* thus synthesized three theories which in England were more distinct or, so to speak, "writ large." Although a delineation of this process qualifies the Burkean correlation, it brings into focus the more important parallel between Doctrinaire and Reform Whig theories of representation. For when the new Charter of 1830 gave legislative initiative to the Chamber and an electoral law in 1831 rewarded the middle class with a "final settlement" which

[17] *Ibid.*, p. 618.   [18] XXXIV (Aug. 1820), 38.
[19] For use of these categories, see Beer, *op. cit., passim*. Their meaning should be self-evident in my discussion below.

doubled the electorate, French *juste milieu* liberalism found itself emerging at a stage quite comparable to the Whiggism of 1832. From this standpoint the seldom explored analogy between the theory of France's 1830 July Revolution and England's 1832 Reform Bill begins to appear fully as meaningful as the conventional 1688–1830 comparison.

First, to return to the Old Whig correlation, the Restoration Chamber neither possessed the legislative initiative of Burke's House of Commons nor represented the interests of the Crown and Peers (in addition to other "legitimate interests") in the direct sense which Burke and later Old Whig theorists like Sir James Mackintosh considered the English Chamber to do.[20] As Royer-Collard put it: "By the words representative government . . . we ought to understand no more than an elective power which concurs with the hereditary powers in the formation of law."[21] Although the Doctrinaires later reversed their position on legislative initiative as well as on ministerial responsibility, they really never adopted the Old Whig view that the lower house should itself be a "virtual replica of the whole three estates" and therefore constitute "the chief virtue and force of the government."[22] Even in Doctrinaire theory of later years it remained the unique role of the King to represent perpetually the "unity, the force, and the independence of the nation."[23] This is clearly reminiscent of the Old Tory notion, dominant in the Tudor-Stuart era, that the King was the initiating, representative head of the corporate community. As for the Chamber of Peers, its distinction in Doctrinaire theory, vis à vis the lower chamber, was to represent those interests "not common to all." In part this was a recognition of the fact of social inequality, for, as Royer-Collard observed, "We are all either peers or commoners." At the same time, the upper

[20] *Ibid.*, pp. 614 ff.   [21] Barante, *op. cit.*, II, 19.
[22] *Edinburgh Review*, X (July 1807), 414–15, theorizing about the House of Commons.   [23] Barante, *op. cit.*, II, 465.

chamber brought to the government that peculiar "principle" embodied in an hereditary peerage: stability.[24]

Secondly, although the Doctrinaires constantly used the term "interests," one is never certain precisely what they meant by it or where they got it. Like "reason," it proves to be a somewhat puzzling category. This ambiguity leads to another departure from Old Whiggism. When either a Tory like Inglis or an Old Whig like Mackintosh spoke of "interest representation," he meant, in addition to the influence of Crown and aristocracy within the House, all classes and orders. That included not only the interests of land, commerce, industry, the great professions, and corporate bodies, but also *"in some places, the lowest classes."* Up through the mid-1820s the Whigs therefore accepted the Tory notion that the only electoral system which could achieve true representation was "a variety of rights of suffrage." They condemned not only universal suffrage, but also any uniform property franchise. The first would place every other interest at the disposal of "ignorant multitudes." The second would inevitably exclude from any representation certain legitimate interests and would scar society with a single humiliating line between electors and nonelectors. In this period the Whigs argued that franchises ought to be patterned differently from one borough to another, ranging from some which were almost democratic to some which were clearly proprietary, so that some members of every class had electoral rights. To quote Mackintosh, the candidates chosen by the particular electors of one place would "virtually" represent "the same sort of people in other places." "The exclusion of the class degrades the whole, but the admission of a part bestows on the whole a sense of importance."[25]

[24] *Ibid.*, pp. 18–19, 34.
[25] Sir James Mackintosh, in the *Edinburgh Review,* XXXI (Dec. 1818), 175–76, 180–83. The article was an answer to Bentham's *Plan of Parliamentary Reform.* See also Brougham, *Contributions,* II, 493.

In contrast, the Doctrinaires not only failed to specify what they meant by "interests," but, perhaps for that very reason, glorified the uniform property qualification which was such an anathema to Tories and to the Whigs of the early 1820s. In comparison with Old Whiggism, Doctrinaire theory thus prescribed a compound virtual representation. Rather than being able to look to the deputy from another district for representation of his interest (e.g., that of a silk-worker), the disenfranchised citizen had to trust the deputy of another *class*.

This brings us to a third departure from Old Whiggism and, at the same time, to the crucial point of intersection between Doctrinaire and Whig theories of representation from the late 1820s on: the middle-class mystique. As perhaps the single most important theme of both the French and English *justes milieux,* the apotheosis of the middle class involved far more than the simple equation between property and reason.

At times the Doctrinaires seemed to see the bourgeoisie simply in an Old Whig sense, as a great new class in society which deserved political status along with other interests. Guizot's criticism of the pre-1832 English rotten borough system was that it had been outmoded by the "progress" of society. The system might have distributed political rights according to capacity during the feudal era, but it excluded the new commercial classes which had long since risen.[26] Again, Royer-Collard declared: "The influence of the middle class is a fact, a potent and formidable fact. . . . The centuries have prepared it; the Revolution has declared it. It is to this class that the new interests belong. Its security cannot be disturbed without imminent danger to the established order."[27]

However, the middle class as an achievement of the centu-

[26] *History of Representative Government,* pp. 396–400.
[27] Barante, *op. cit.,* I, 456; also II, 134.

ries led easily to an image of the class not as just a new interest, but as an almost mystical repository of *all* the true interests, virtues, and history of the nation. For Guizot the advent of this "new general class," dating from the rise of the free cities during the middle ages, constituted the master clue to European history. Speaking in the late 1820s he anticipated the language of Marx:

The . . . great result of the enfranchisement of the cities was the struggle of classes: a struggle which constitutes the very fact of modern history, and of which it is full.

Modern Europe, indeed, is born of this struggle between the different classes of society. . . . The struggle, instead of rendering society stationary, has been a principal cause of its progress.[28]

Unlike Marx, Guizot did not believe that the struggle had meant the successive destruction of one class by another. On the contrary, the struggle had involved "the necessity of combating and yielding by turns; a variety of interests, passions, and excitements; the desire to conquer without the power to do so." And from all this had come the genius of European civilization. Whatever "strong moral hostility" the struggle had produced, all classes had nevertheless "progressively approached, assimilated, and understood each other." Again the sovereignty of reason! The great achievement of this modern era was a "certain public mind, a certain community of interests, of ideas, of sentiments" which had emerged in "every country of Europe."[29]

It was quite clear in Doctrinaire theory that the very middle class which had initiated the long struggle was now a microcosm of this "certain public mind." With the war of classes at an end, the middle-class elector represented perfectly the citizen below him in the social scale. "He does not exclude him, he represents him, he protects him, he covers

[28] *History of Civilization in Europe,* p. 184.
[29] *Ibid.*

him, he experiences and defends the same interests."[30] Like Marx's proletariat, the chosen class of the *juste milieu* now bore the ultimate destiny of society. *"All the interests* find there their natural representation." To this was added the Aristotelian notion that the middle class is more virtuous, more moderate than either the upper or the lower. "Above is a certain desire to dominate, against which it is necessary to guard; below, ignorance . . . complete incapacity."[31]

The Reform Whigs in England reached the middle-class mystique by a remarkably similar route. As long as they accepted the Old Whig premises, their quarrel with the Tories was simply that the pre-1832 electoral system did not conform to the standards of that theory. Granted that lack of uniformity was a sound principle, it was nonsense, said Brougham, to argue that "all classes and interests" were properly represented when as many as 250 of 658 seats were at the disposal of local "patrons" and when rotten boroughs like Old Sarum sent two members each to Commons, while the burgeoning new industrial centers of Birmingham, Leeds, Manchester, and Sheffield had not a single member. The truth was that "many vast branches of the community" were "wholly deprived of all share in their representation."[32] Gui-

[30] Guizot, *Histoire Parlementaire,* III, 556.

[31] Barante, *op. cit.,* I, 290 (italics mine).

[32] Brougham, in the *Edinburgh Review,* XX (Nov. 1812), 418. The crazy-quilt pattern of the pre-1832 British electoral system has been so often and exhaustively described that it is scarcely necessary here to detail the wide variety of borough franchises. For a definitive work, see Edward and A. G. Porritt, *The Unreformed House of Commons* (2 vols.: Cambridge University Press, 1903). For shorter treatments see Halévy, *History of the English People,* I, 108 ff.; Butler, *op. cit.,* pp. 174 ff.; and Walter Bagehot, "History of the Unreformed Parliament," *Works* (Hartford: Travelers Insurance Co., 1889), IV, 369 ff. Accounts vary in placing the precise number of proprietary seats, depending on what degree of control by the patron is considered sufficient to render a borough "proprietary"; 250 seems a reasonable estimate. In 1827 the Tory John Wilson Croker put the figure at 276 (*The Croker Papers* [New York: Scribner's, 1884], I, 342).

zot was right. If the old system had been appropriate for the England of three or four centuries ago, that England had long since been buried. Just as in Doctrinaire theory, the master clue to the Whigs' "new England" was the middle class. It was the locus not only of vast new forms of property and interests, but also of "respectability" and "knowledge . . . unexampled in former times."[33] Thus the only just solution could be to admit "the great body of the middle orders to a share in government."[34] Far from causing political revolution, this would really "restore" the Old Whig pattern of representing all classes. More than that, it would avoid an otherwise inevitable revolution. "In all ages," declared Macaulay, "a chief cause of intestine disorders of states has been that the natural distribution . . . and the legal distribution of power have not corresponded with each other. This is no newly discovered truth. It was well known to Aristotle more than 2000 years ago."[35] Reestablish Aristotelian proportional equality and England would be saved!

Just as in France, however, the Whig *juste milieu* theorists often claimed far more than that the middle class was simply a great new interest to be absorbed in the Old Whig order. If they started with that premise, they ended by portraying the middle class as superior to all others—they defined it as a "general class" in the same sense that the Doctrinaires theorized. Although the Whigs did not match Guizot's articulate historical treatment of this theme, the gist of their argument was the same. Even before 1820 Mackintosh had somewhat qualified his rejection of a uniform franchise by conceding that if elective influence had to be limited to "one order," the honor should go to the middle class. Why? Because that class

[33] Brougham, *Contributions,* II, 501; also Macaulay, *Miscellanies,* I, 5 (in House of Commons, March 2, 1831).

[34] *Ibid.,* p. 72 (in House of Commons, Dec. 16, 1831).

[35] *Ibid.,* p. 94 (in House of Commons, Feb. 28, 1832). For Brougham's "restore the old order" theme, see his *Speeches* (Philadelphia: Lea and Blanchard, 1841), II, 45 (in House of Lords, Oct. 7, 1831).

had the "largest share of sense and virtue" and "the most numerous connections of interest with other parts of society."[36] From the mid-1820s on this theme clearly began to supersede the Old Whig idea of a diversity of interests. By 1829 Macaulay was calling the middling classes "the natural representatives of the human race," whose interest was "identical with that of the innumerable generations to follow." His fervent wish was for a reform which would make the Commons "the express image of the middle orders of Britain."[37] The *Manchester Guardian* insisted that the middle class "never can have any interest adverse . . . to those below them in society."[38] And the *Edinburgh Review* declared that, in fact, the middle classes *were* "the country."[39] This was an equation which Brougham embellished in his famous eulogy:

But if there is a mob, there is the people also. I speak now of the middle classes—of those hundreds of thousands of respectable persons—the most numerous and by far the most wealthy order in the community . . . who are also the genuine depositories of sober, rational, intelligent, and honest English feeling.[40]

The obvious result of the middle-class mystique was to undercut the Old Whig idea of variety franchise. If the middle class were indeed the magic common denominator of society, the job, in Macaulay's words, was simply "to draw the line in such a manner that every decent farmer and shopkeeper might possess the elective franchise."[41] And that was precisely what the Great Reform Bill purported to do by

[36] In the *Edinburgh Review*, XXXI (Dec. 1818), 191–92.

[37] "Mill's Essay on Government," *Essays*, II, 42; "Utilitarian Theory of Government," *Essays*, II, 131.

[38] Quoted in Butler, *op. cit.*, p. 263.   [39] LII (Jan. 1831), 544.

[40] Brougham, *Speeches*, II, 41. Even reform "aristocrats" like Grey joined the chorus by calling the middle classes "the real and efficient mass of public opinion" (Trevelyan, *op. cit.*, p. 313).

[41] "Utilitarian Theory of Government," *Essays*, II, 131.

enfranchising, in the boroughs, the "occupiers," whether owners or tenants, of buildings with an annual rental value of ten pounds or more. That line, and not the extensive disenfranchisements of rotten boroughs under schedules "A" and "B," was the really revolutionary feature of the Bill. For it not only shifted the emphasis from a variety to a uniformity of franchise. It also set a precedent for eventually drawing an even lower uniform line which would admit, en masse, the next class below.[42]

In a more immediate sense the uniform ten-pound borough franchise also subverted the magic idea of "virtual representation" which had made variety suffrage tolerable. If there was any truth in that idea, there was really no need to swamp the electorate with the entire middle class—just a part would have done. But Macaulay made short shrift of this: "Now, Sir, I do not understand how a power which is salutary when exercised virtually can be noxious when exercised directly. . . . The utmost that can be expected from virtual representation is that it may be as good as direct. . . . If so, why not grant direct representation to places which, as everybody allows, ought . . . to be represented?"[43] This, in fact, was exactly what the Radicals had always thought of Old Whiggism—that it was a "fallacy" and "sophism."[44] Macaulay was thus granting a dangerous

---

[42] As Disraeli wrote in *Coningsby,* bk. I, chap. VII, the ten-pound borough franchise "virtually conceded the principle of universal suffrage." Bagehot developed the same theme in "Parliamentary Reform" (*Works,* IV, 291 ff.). It should be noted, however, that despite the general uniformity of the new ten-pound franchise, some of the even more liberal franchises which had existed in the relatively few "open" constituencies before 1832 were continued during the lifetime of their possessors. In other instances those franchises were extinguished by the Bill. For a detailed survey of these marginal intricacies, see Norman Gash, *Politics in the Age of Peel* (London: Longmans, 1953), pp. 86 ff.

[43] *Miscellanies,* I, 9–10 (in House of Commons, March 2, 1831).

[44] For example, the *Westminster Review,* IV (July 1825), 214–15; XII (Jan. 1830), 222–26.

premise when he declared that all who deserved representation ought to vote. Actually the 1832 assumption that the middle class was a "general class" was a claim that *it* virtually represented all classes. And how could virtual representation be wrong *within* a class, but right *between* classes? From this standpoint Tories like John Wilson Croker who scoffed, "moderate reform . . . moderate gunpowder," were expressing something more than party rhetoric.[45]

All this, however, was a danger which the "men of '32" vehemently denied. Although the Whigs were surely not so naive as to think that the middle-class settlement would last forever, the words "final" and "permanent" occurred over and over in their arguments for reform, duplicating the view which the Doctrinaires took of the enlarged 200-franc franchise established by the new electoral law after the July Revolution. What was the rationale behind the theme of "finality"? At times the Whigs seemed to argue, in tactical terms, that only the assurance of a lasting settlement would win adequate support for the large degree of reform they desired; but on other occasions they reversed this logic by claiming that only "a decisive and extensive measure" would produce "permanent contentment."[46]

On both sides of the Channel, however, the two crucial premises behind "finality" were a terror of rule by the mob and a faith in the openness of the middle class. Both reveal the impact of Revolution on the *juste milieu* theory of representation. Both are also a further illustration of the peculiar characteristics of the middling mind which have already been suggested. To regard the middle-class franchise as only tentative would be an invitation to universal suffrage. And that, said Guizot, would be the "death of liberty as well as order."[47] Despite the very real differences in English and

[45] *The Croker Papers,* I, 497.
[46] Macaulay, *Miscellanies,* I, 32 (in House of Commons, July 5, 1831).
[47] *Histoire Parlementaire,* V, 214; also III, 561.

French politics, Macaulay was equally fearful and seemed once again to be conjuring up the specter of rather more serious danger than the Whig *juste milieu* in fact faced. For Macaulay, nothing could come of universal suffrage except "one vast spoilation." Nor did he limit that proposition to the context of Europe. "As for America, we appeal to the 20th century."[48]

On the other hand, the genius of the middle-class franchise was that it would automatically adjust to the "progress of society." What his critics too often forget is that even Guizot's notorious "Enrichissez-vous" was more than a pure crudity. He repeatedly described the middle class as an open class "without privileges, without monopolies." It was "incessantly supplied by recruits from the bulk of the population." Only the "dull, lazy, or licentious" should fail to rise. In turn, those who became recruits to the middle class would also become recruits to the electorate.[49] As Macaulay implied, even the "mob" might one day become ten-pound occupiers: "We shall make our institutions more democratic . . . not by lowering the franchise to the level of the great mass of the community, but by raising . . . the great mass up to the level of the franchise."[50]

If the *juste milieu* view of universal suffrage reflected fear of the Revolution, this theory of the openness of the middle class was also homage to one of its ideals: privilege must never again bar talent. More than that, this theory also seemed to involve that strange faith which the *juste milieu*

[48] *Miscellanies*, I, 274 (in House of Commons, May 3, 1842); also "Mill's Essay on Government," *Essays*, II, 37, 40. Reviewing de Tocqueville's *Democracy in America* in the *Edinburgh Review*, LXXII (Oct. 1840), 14, John Stuart Mill had a rather more interesting explanation of American democracy: "America is *all* middle class; the whole people being in a condition, both as to education and pecuniary means, corresponding to the middle classes here."

[49] *Histoire Parlementaire*, II, 223, and III, 105, 107; *Democracy in France* (New York: Appleton, 1849), p. 51; and *Mémoires*, VIII, 522.

[50] *Miscellanies*, II, 182–83 (at Edinburgh, Nov. 2, 1852).

mind retains in the power of sweet reasonableness at the very moment that it warns of the dangerous extremes which confront the middle ground. For the logic of the Guizot-Macaulay argument was that the middle class would inexorably universalize itself through the extension of "prudence" and "intelligence" to all sectors of society. Thus their theory of representation carried the same promise which we have seen in their theory of sovereignty: the very extremes which made the *juste milieu* a relevant center would somehow succumb in the end to the march of reason. And that amounted to a claim that the *juste milieu* was realistic as well as relevant.

Interestingly enough, the promise of a middle class which will universalize itself suggests still another correlation with the Marxist concept of the proletariat. Not only is the middle class of *juste milieu* theory the product of a long, tortuous historical process of class struggle. Not only does it bear all the legitimate interests and ultimate destiny of society at large. But it also promises a future in which the idea of class will become irrelevant. As with Marxism, after all the class emphasis, the final goal is to dissolve class by realizing a utopia of individualism. In this sense the class analysis of both Marx and the *juste milieu* was a new route back to an old dream world: back to the heavenly city of the eighteenth century.

Social Reality

Nothing is more striking in Doctrinaire theory than the lack of any hardheaded examination of the social reality which was assumed to lie behind the image of the "general class." The theory seemed to presume that the bourgeoisie possessed remarkable vitality, a sense of collective unity, and a unique integrative capacity in society at large. Yet all we are given from start to finish are sweeping generalizations about the messianic rise of that class in history, vague references to the "commercial" and "industrial" orders, and the description of "a class to whom manual toil is not necessary, which does not live by wages."[51] Beyond that the Doctrinaires leave us to take it largely on faith that there was, in fact, a class in French society corresponding to their vision.

It is interesting that although Guizot's middle class seemed to be the rightful successor to *le tier état* of Sièyes and the Revolution, Guizot himself often preferred another catch phrase, *le pays légal,* to describe the blessed circle of those who enjoyed the franchise. And I would suggest that the narrow, artificial implications of that expression are a revealing contrast to the expansive, emotional appeal of Sièyes' battle cry a generation earlier. For the truth is that however much Guizot rationalized his chosen class in terms that did homage to the ideals of the Revolution, neither he nor the bourgeoisie ever cut completely free from the values of the Ancien Regime. Indeed, in the very process of revolting against the old order, the bourgeoisie had somehow acquired a curious craving to legitimize *itself* as a new aristocracy. It was not satisfied to be just a great new interest, or even a "general class." In Ruggiero's words, "it now wanted *s'ennoblir.*"[52] However much the Doctrinaires talked of social mobility, *juste milieu* individualism remained a strangely unfulfilled dream. The Ancien Regime had burned the experience of caste too deeply into bourgeois consciousness. The result was a kind of schizophrenia in which the bourgeoisie saw itself on the one hand as an open, universal class, while on the other hand it sought the trappings of nobility, worshipped landed property, and instinctively particularized itself.

This schizophrenia was only one aspect of a disintegration

[51] Guizot, *Histoire Parlementaire,* III, 104; "Élections," *Discours Académiques,* pp. 389–90.   [52] *Op. cit.,* p. 169.

which had become obvious throughout French society long before the Revolution. De Tocqueville and others have often placed the source of that disintegration in the nature of the French aristocracy: a class possessing rank, but not talent, and enjoying privilege without responsibility. Exempt from the *taille,* the basic direct tax of the realm, as well as other burdens, the nobility not only refused the task of local administration, but deserted the provinces and land for the court life of Versailles and Paris. If the French peasant more often owned his land than the English peasant, that very fact made all the more oppressive the tremendous general tax increases before the Revolution and, more particularly, the *droits de franc fief,* payments which the Crown exacted from the commoner who purchased a fief, but not from the noble. The understandable result of all this was a continuing estrangement of the aristocracy from the peasantry.[53]

An equally serious estrangement was that of aristocracy from the rising middle class. For one thing, the doctrine of "derogation" had for centuries meant that any member of the aristocracy who engaged in commerce or industry suffered loss of nobility for himself and issue. Although some have traced this rule to early bourgeois demands that the nobility compensate for its privileges by not competing in trade, by the eighteenth century few nobles chafed under the disability. Rather, they considered it a credential of their own superiority and looked with disdain on bourgeois callings. In turn this disdain gradually filtered into the bourgeoisie itself.[54]

[53] De Tocqueville, *The Old Regime and the French Revolution,* trans. Gilbert Stuart (New York: Doubleday Anchor, 1955), pp. 102 ff., 125 ff.; Franklin Ford, *Robe and Sword* (Harvard University Press, 1953), pp. 27–29; Georges Lefebvre, *The Coming of the French Revolution,* trans. R. R. Palmer (New York: Vintage Books, 1957), pp. 9, 21 ff.; de Ruggiero, *op. cit.,* p. 4.

[54] Concerning the origin and effect of derogation, see Ford, *op. cit.,* pp. 25–26; Frantz Funck-Brentano, *The Old Regime in France* (London: Longmans, 1929), pp. 88–89; Elinor G. Barber, *The Bourgeoisie in 18th Century France* (Princeton University Press, 1955), p. 60; and Lefebvre, *op. cit.,* p. 14.

Even more important was the fact that the bourgeoisie, with the peasantry, suffered the full weight of taxation, military service, and other burdens which the nobility escaped. If the peasant simply continued to suffer, it is true that the more adaptable urban bourgeois soon found a means of self-protection: the purchase of official administrative posts which carried exemptions from these burdens and also exonerated the bourgeois from the stigma of trade. Often such offices provided an even more complete escape by conferring nobility either on the new holder or his descendants. For the commoner of requisite wealth, ennoblement could also be acquired directly through the purchase of "letters of patent" from the financially hard-pressed Crown. Although bourgeois flight to public office and nobility was fairly frequent, it was not foolproof, since the Crown often practiced virtual extortion by revoking previous purchases, leaving the victims little alternative but costly repurchase.[55]

But this pattern of privilege and disability had far more serious consequences for the French bourgeoisie than extortion. First, the immunities enjoyed by even the bourgeois content with nonennobling office alienated him from other orders in society—especially the peasantry—and tended to make the bourgeoisie a "pseudo-aristocracy." Second, these same privileges, all of varying ranks, splintered the bourgeoisie itself into what de Tocqueville called "an immense number of separate elements," each with its own particular status and prerogatives.[56] "Nothing was more pronounced than the ordering of ranks within the bourgeoisie itself."[57] This was the beginning of that curious development which, as Rémond puts it, was eventually to give both Balzac's César Birotteau and Stendhal's rich M. Leuwen *père* such highly incongruous claims to the adjective "bourgeois."[58]

[55] Ford, *op. cit.*, pp. 12–13; Barber, *op. cit.*, pp. 106 ff.; de Tocqueville, *op. cit.*, pp. 63, 88.

[56] *Ibid.*, pp. 39, 94, 115, 136.

[57] Lefebvre, *op. cit.*, p. 40; also Barber, *op. cit.*, pp. 59, 141 ff.

[58] *Op. cit.*, p. 77.

Third, and most significant, the bourgeois desire to invest capital and effort in public office and ennoblement subverted the very commercial-industrial values of productivity, risk, and competition which are ordinarily associated with the middle class. If the typical petit bourgeois was content with the security of a modest post and safe investment in land, the more ambitious bourgeois was often a "tax farmer" who collected indirect taxes on a concession from the Crown, paying the government a fixed amount and pocketing the rest—hardly an enterprise of "risk" or "productivity."[59] The *most* ambitious bourgeois—who would seem the likeliest to become a self-sufficient entrepreneur—was paradoxically the least interested in such an achievement. The *summum bonum* for him was ennoblement. This meant, once his wealth was adequate, that middle-class values were more than stunted; they became taboo and he himself left the rest of society behind. "Once a man crossed . . . he was cut off from the outside." "Never had the gap between the middle class and the nobility been so great."[60]

When one moves from the age of the Ancien Regime to that of *juste milieu,* he cannot help but see the truth of de Tocqueville's remark that, despite the Great Revolution and Napoleonic Wars, the society of the new century was very

[59] Lefebvre, *op. cit.,* pp. 36–38; de Tocqueville, *op. cit.,* p. 24; Maurice Halbwachs, *The Psychology of Social Class* (London: Heinemann, 1958), pp. 40–42; and B. de Jouvenel, "Treatment of Capitalism by Continental Historians," in *Capitalism and the Historians,* F. A. von Hayek, ed. (Chicago University Press, 1954), p. 112. For a recent reexamination of the eighteenth-century bourgeoisie, see Alfred Cobban, *The Social Interpretation of the French Revolution* (Cambridge University Press, 1964), pp. 36–67, 162–73. Cobban's argument is not only that the bourgeoisie was exceedingly complex in structure, but also that the very bourgeois elements which led the Revolution were deeply hostile to commercial-industrial values. Indeed, in what is a revision of a major theme of Lefebvre, he concludes that the Revolution was in no real sense a triumph for those values, but rather for the interests of landowners, large and small.

[60] De Tocqueville, *op. cit.,* p. 89.

largely a reconstruction from "the debris of the old order."[61] Or, as Alfred Cobban remarks, one is "most struck by the permanent elements in the French social pattern . . . a society with many new elements it is true, but bearing on it like a palimpsest the inadequately effaced writing of the Ancien Regime."[62] For once again, in the France of Louis Philippe, practically all the old bourgeois traits appear. The craving for investment in land is as strong as ever. The bourgeois desire for public office is, if anything, stronger, with Guizot's bureaucracy approaching his precious *pays légal* in size. Envy and mimicry of aristocracy, disdain of trade, industry, and money per se, reliance on the state for protection from risk, emphasis on luxury consumption—all these continue to be hallmarks of the bourgeois character.[63] When Samuel Smiles' celebrated book *Self Help* became a best seller in the England of 1859, what complaint did the French reviewers have? That the title was really *untranslatable* in French![64]

French novels of the era are a fascinating window into the bourgeois soul. True, of all the human vices, probably none receives a fuller share of attention than greed for money. Balzac's Grandet is perhaps the classic miser of all literature. In Stendhal's village of Verrières, "yielding a return is the consideration which settles everything."[65] M. de Vaize could

[61] *Ibid.*, p. vii; see also his *The European Revolution and Correspondence with Gobineau*, trans. John Lukacs (New York: Doubleday Anchor, 1959), p. 152.

[62] *Op. cit.*, p. 169.

[63] De Tocqueville, *The European Revolution*, pp. 151–53; Charles Morazé, *La France Bourgeoise* (Paris: Librairie Armand Colin, 1946), pp. 84 ff.; J. B. Christopher, "The Desiccation of the Bourgeois Spirit," in *Modern France*, E. M. Earle, ed. (Princeton University Press, 1951), pp. 44 ff.; François Bourricaud, "France," in *Institutions of Advanced Societies*, Arnold M. Rose, ed. (University of Minnesota Press, 1958), pp. 476 ff., 512 ff.; Cobban, *op. cit.*, pp. 68–80.

[64] See Asa Briggs, "Introduction" to *Self Help* (London: John Murray, 1958), p 26.

[65] *The Red and the Black*, trans. C. K. Scott Moncrieff (New York: Modern Library, 1926), I, chap. 2, p. 16.

not feel "truly a minister" until he had made a few thousand francs in a crooked stock market deal.[66] Yet nothing is clearer than that money alone could not legitimize the French bourgeoisie in either its own eyes or those of the aristocracy. Since 1815 M. de Rênal has "blushed at his connection with industry," is now preoccupied with outdoing Valenod's possession of two Norman horses by hiring a tutor for his children, and has succumbed to the "landowning mania" by acquiring extensive gardens and a four-towered castle.[67] Even the young Lucien Leuwen's dazzling wealth is not enough. "If half his real merit could be exchanged for an inherited position . . . he would be good for something in society."[68] After acquiring both noble husband and name, Mme. la Maréchale de Fervaques still "seemed to have no other object than to make people forget that she was the daughter of an *industriel.*"[69]

Aside from Balzac's own financial misfortunes, one might suggest that his fascination with bankruptcy may also reflect the peculiar inability of bourgeois thrift to cope with the hazards of "aristocratic tastes." If César Birotteau seems a sound bourgeois when he talks of avoiding "excessive expenditure," he is, significantly, engaged in the trade of perfume. In turn, César's own bankruptcy is presaged by his extravagant ball to celebrate a decoration from the King, and is accomplished by a disastrous speculation in real estate. Old Goriot, after prudently accumulating a fortune as a vermicelli maker, has no other ambition than to purchase noble marriages for his two daughters. Having achieved that, he is then driven to heartbreak by exclusion from his daughters' homes and to financial ruin by their continued pleas for more

[66] Stendhal, *Lucien Leuwen, Book Two, The Telegraph,* trans. Louise Varèse (New York: New Directions, 1950), chap. 5, p. 50.

[67] *The Red and the Black,* I, chap. 1, pp. 11–12, chap. 3, pp. 21–22, chap. 8, p. 67.

[68] *Lucien Leuwen, Book Two, The Telegraph,* chap. 13, p. 137.

[69] *The Red and the Black,* II, chap. 54, p. 211.

and more money with which to satisfy the costly tastes of aristocratic fashion. In the end Goriot dies without a cent and is buried in a pauper's grave, unattended by either daughter. Grandet, whose brother is ruined by the lures of Parisian society, manages to avoid a similar fate, but not without being a pathological miser. The bourgeois alternatives, Balzac seems to imply, are either seduction by aristocracy or sterility. If one is looking for symbolism, Grandet's daughter inherits his vast estate intact, but marries M. de Bonfons only on the agreement that the marriage will not be consummated.

As Goriot's fate suggests, bourgeois worship of aristocratic values continues to be an agent not of social integration, but of disintegration and isolation. To turn again to Stendhal, the dominant mood of French society a full half-century after the Revolution is still "the resentment of rank against merit."[70] Society remains "torn by violent schisms."[71] The "walls" with which M. de Rênal assiduously encloses his property are, in a deeper sense, the ramparts between privilege and unprivilege. The subtitle "The Telegraph" is not a symbol of social communication, but rather of rigged elections and dishonest bourse speculation made easy. Why are the two heroes, Julien Sorel and Lucien Leuwen, both *déclassé,* the first obviously and bitterly, the second somewhat subtly and happily? Quite simply because no one class—certainly not the bourgeoisie—has the greatness to yield a hero. No one class holds together or transcends the others. No one class rewards talent with congruous status or respect. Whatever his milieu—peasantry, the de Rênal bourgeois household, the Church seminary, or the Hôtel de la Mole—Julien senses always that he is in a closed compartment, isolated from the rest of society. Lucien, born to the cream of "la

[70] *Lucien Leuwen, Book One, The Green Huntsman,* trans. Louise Varèse (New York: New Directions, 1950), chap. 17, p. 189.
[71] *Ibid.,* chap. 11, p. 132.

grande bourgeoisie," experiences the same frustration. Republican by inclination, *juste milieu* by family, and the lover of a noblewoman, his very reasonableness makes him suspect in every camp as a spy from elsewhere. His own hero is most appropriately Talleyrand, another talented *déclassé* figure who both served and used all camps.[72]

Against this societal background the Doctrinaire vision of the bourgeoisie is revealed for what it was: sheer illusion. If it is even accurate to label as a "class" the disparate array of people and groups claiming the title "bourgeois,"[73] this was

[72] Flaubert's Frederic Moreau is another illustration. In the end, Frederic looks on life in general much as he had looked on the Revolution of 1848: "There are situations in which a man of the least cruel disposition is so much detached from his fellow-man that he would see the entire human race perishing without a single throb of the heart" (*Sentimental Education* [Akron: St. Dunston, 1904], II, chap. 13, p. 108). For general treatment of this theme in Stendhal, Balzac, and Flaubert, see Raymond Giraud, *The Unheroic Hero* (Rutgers University Press, 1957).

[73] Perhaps it is not, if one accepts Talcott Parsons' description of a "class" as an integrated group whose member "kinship units . . . are approximately equally valued" (*Essays in Sociological Theory* [Glencoe, Ill.: Free Press, 1954], p. 77). See also G. D. H. Cole's view of the middle class as a relatively homogeneous, integrated social stratum lying between two other strata in a "unitary social structure" ("The Conception of the Middle Classes," *The British Journal of Sociology*, I, [Dec. 1950], 275 ff.). By Cole's historical analysis the middle class would seem a result as well as a cause of the industrial revolution. For it was that revolution which restructured the plurality of the old feudal corporate order into a three-tier society consisting of remnants of the old aristocracy on top, a class conscious bourgeoisie in the middle, and a lower class of urban and rural laborers who were beginning to have a feeling of common cause. Cole's approach would seem far more adequate than the definition which excludes at the outset all manual labor and all nobility, and then labels as the middle class the multifarious array of occupations which remain. For example, R. L. and A. Maude, *The English Middle Classes* (New York: Knopf, 1950), pp. 8–9; F. C. Palm, *The Middle Classes, Then and Now* (New York: Macmillan, 1936), pp. 4–5. For one thing, many of these nonnoble, nonmanual callings had existed for centuries before the industrial revolution without being considered either a "class" or in the "middle" of anything. As Asa Briggs has shown, it was only from the late eighteenth century on that the phrases "class" and "middle class" came into common parlance. (See his "Middle Class Consciousness in English

then a class which disbelieved in itself in the midst of a society which shared that disbelief. Nor was it any of the other things that the Doctrinaires claimed. It was hardly "without privileges, without monopolies." Its commitment to the great "new forms of property" was deeply ambivalent. Above all, it was surely not a "general class" which could integrate and represent the interests of society at large. The irony was that the very theorists who are invariably accused as apologists for class interest were idealizing a class which, in a sense, did not even exist! Once again, just as with the sovereignty of reason, Doctrinaire theory proves not a reflection of reality, but a dream fantasy.

Even the "inherent" quality which the French theory of the middle class at first seemed to have must be qualified. For the test of an inherent, vis à vis positional, ideology is not simply to *ask* the question "who?" rather than "where?" Surely the test should be the *answer*. And when one looks from the Doctrinaire image of the general class to the bourgeoisie itself, the answer is unsatisfactory enough to make one wonder if "where?" is not the more relevant question. And I think that that question is also the easier to answer. For from first to last, the job was to hold "une ligne à égale distance de droite et de gauche."[74] Whether the Doctrinaires realized it or not, their theory of the middle class disguised as an inherent ideal what was in large measure a positional commitment to maintain that line. In turn, whether Guizot himself realized it or not, the artificial implications of his favorite catch phrase, *le pays légal,* were to stand confirmed in the end. For *le pays légal* turned out to be little more than a contrived construct representing not social reality, but rather political strategy. And as we will see when we come to

---

Politics, 1780–1846," *Past and Present,* I, [April 1956], pp. 65 ff.; and "The Language of 'Class' in Early 19th Century England," in *Essays in Labour History,* Asa Briggs and John Saville, eds. [London: Macmillan, 1960], pp. 43 ff.)   [74] Faguet's phrase, *op. cit.,* p. 307.

the politics of the July Regime, that strategy was itself fully as illusive as the Doctrinaire view of society.

If it is fair to say that the Doctrinaires' sovereignty of reason tacitly mistook French for English politics, it is perhaps equally fair to say that the middle-class mystique mistook French for English society. When one turns to England, the background of the eighteenth century is again important. Instead of an aristocracy of privilege without responsibility, the English ruling class had long been celebrated for assuming the heaviest burdens of taxation and diligently discharging the duties of local as well as national government. Instead of a rigidly compartmentalized society, one finds an impressive degree of peaceful interpenetration between landed aristocracy and the emerging middle class of traders and manufacturers. In contrast with France, where each son of a noble inherited a title and was barred from trade, in England only the eldest son acquired the title. From this resulted that practice which so surprised Voltaire on his visit to England: the apprenticing of a virtual army of younger sons of the aristocracy not only to the professions, but to trade and industry as well.[75]

As has often been observed, in France the word "gentleman" meant neither more nor less than a nobleman; in eigtheenth-century England, however, the word had a far more general meaning which included almost anyone whose mode of life embodied a certain standard of material comfort, fair dealing, and education. To repeat Defoe's famous remark, "trade is so far here from being inconsistent with a gentleman, that in short trade in England makes a gentleman, and has peopled the nation with gentlemen."[76] It also seems certain that the man who became a gentleman through

[75] W. E. H. Lecky, *History of England in the 18th Century* (New York, 1878), V, 311–12.

[76] Quoted in L. B. Namier, *England in the Age of the American Revolution* (London: Macmillan, 1930), p. 10.

trade had far easier access to the aristocracy than the French bourgeois. It was not that the English aristocracy held open house. It was rather, in de Tocqueville's expression, that the barriers were so ill defined "that you never knew when you had got there" and "everyone who hovered on its outskirts nursed the agreeable illusion that he belonged to it."[77]

As Defoe's remark implies, the important clue to this pattern of social mobility was the pervasive acceptance in English society of the very commercial-industrial values which were so scorned in France. England's lead over France in industrialization was not just the result of the effort of one class. In the deepest sense it was a national effort. Even the Hammonds, who may sometimes have overemphasized class antagonisms, declared, "In 18th century England . . . industry seemed the most important thing in the world. *All classes* put industrial expansion high among the objects of public policy."[78]

As a result of the enclosure movement which combined the old "open fields" and thousands of small yeoman holdings into large-scale farms, even agriculture became virtually a form of capitalism, with landowners more and more oriented toward commercial profit at distant markets. The common practice of entailing land and the rule of primogeniture compounded this trend by tending to keep the great estates resulting from enclosure intact from one generation to another. Again the contrast with France is interesting. There, minute subdivision of land was encouraged not only by the ambition of every commoner to own a small plot, but also by the less general application of primogeniture.[79]

[77] *The Old Regime,* pp. 88–89; also 59–60.
[78] J. L. and B. Hammond, *The Rise of Modern Industry* (New York: Harcourt, Brace, 1926), pp. 64–65 (italics mine).
[79] J. H. Clapham, *An Economic History of Modern Britain: The Early Railway Age, 1820–50* (Cambridge University Press, 1955), pp. 15 ff., 30, 98 ff.; E. Cecil, *Primogeniture: A Short History of Its Development in Various Countries and Its Practical Effects* (London, 1895), pp. 91–94.

In the nineteenth century this pattern of social mobility and commitment to the middle-class values of productivity, acquisitiveness, and risk is even more striking. De Tocqueville arrived in England in 1833 expecting to find the country on the brink of "a great revolution."[80] He was instead impressed, as was Taine a quarter-century later, by the continuing consensus of English society and the openness of the aristocracy. As de Tocqueville put it, the English had a genius for blending the "spirit of association and the spirit of exclusion." The secret was not far to find: English society represented a system of "removable inequalities." Even "the aristocracy is founded on wealth, a thing which may be acquired, and not on birth which cannot be."[81] Both de Tocqueville and Taine sensed that the *summum bonum,* in contrast with France, was neither land nor ennoblement, but simply money per se. "To make money . . . is . . . the all absorbing idea."[82] There was neither more nor less than a "cult of money."[83] One might even mistake Birmingham for America![84]

These same insights are richly developed in Anthony Trollope's vast panorama of Victorian society. Probably more reliable than a master of caricature like Dickens or a moralist like Eliot, Trollope is invariably praised for his skill in "detecting slight social differences" and "subtle degrees of rank."[85] That very reputation implies a truth about the society

[80] *Journeys to England and Ireland,* trans. George Lawrence and K. P. Mayer (London: Faber and Faber, 1958), p. 66.

[81] *Ibid.,* pp. 15, 58–60, 67, 88.

[82] Hippolyte Taine, *Notes on England,* trans. Edward Hyams (Fair Lawn, N.J.: Essential Books, 1958), p. 190.

[83] De Tocqueville, *Journeys,* pp. 90–91, 115. Granted that Taine and de Tocqueville may have been overstating this point, the contrast with France must nevertheless have been impressive to lead them to do so. For an interesting chapter on the "commercial spirit," see W. E. Houghton, *The Victorian Frame of Mind* (Yale University Press, 1957), pp. 183–95.

[84] De Tocqueville, *Journeys,* p. 94.

[85] Although Trollope's major works date from the decade after 1848, the middle period of the century has, in England, such deep unity that their value for this study seems unimpaired. In fact it may be enhanced—

he depicted: however many "rankings" it might still include, they were generally subtle rather than sharp, and the highest were yielding gradually but inevitably to the world of trade and industry. Arabella de Courcy had not only reconciled herself to a "commoner" for the compensation of a "fine fortune," but she also assured her son in turn that were poor, illegitimate Mary Thorne an heiress, "the world would forgive her birth on account of her wealth." When Mary actually proves to be nothing less than an heiress, Lady Arabella is the first to welcome her to Greshamsbury as "dear Mary."[86] Again, though the son of a tailor, Mr. Moffat would do very well for Augusta Gresham. "Mr. Moffat has that which ranks above family honors. He is a very rich man."[87] With "great wealth" Sir Damask Monogram had even "got over the difficulty of being the grandson of a butcher."[88] And granted that Sir Felix Carbury must "marry money," what did it matter who Marie Melmotte's mother had been?[89]

Just as significant as aristocracy's self-debasement before Mammon is Mammon's refusal to be seduced by aristocracy. Trollope's *nouveau,* Miss Dunstable, heiress to an immense fortune, looks only with amusement and indifference upon her various titled suitors.[90] Mr. Moffat, rebelling at "the great cost" of aristocratic tastes, shows little hesitation in jilting Augusta when he sees elsewhere the prospect of an alliance

---

by suggesting the relative permanence of the societal consensus behind the terms of 1832. For commentary on Trollope, see Asa Briggs, *Victorian People* (University of Chicago Press, 1955), pp. 87 ff.; Michael Sadleir, *Anthony Trollope* (New York: Houghton Mifflin, 1927); John H. Wildman, *Anthony Trollope's England* (Brown University Press, 1940); and O. J. Cockshut, *Anthony Trollope, A Critical Study* (London: Collins, 1955).

[86] *Doctor Thorne* (New York: Dodd, Mead, 1909), I, chap. 1, p. 7, and II, chap. 16, p. 253, chap. 24, pp. 372 ff.

[87] *Ibid.,* I, chap. 4, p. 76, chap. 7, p. 122.

[88] *The Way We Live Now* (New York: Knopf, 1950), chap. 32, p. 262.

[89] *Ibid.,* chap. 2, pp. 12, 18, chap. 3, p. 22.

[90] *Doctor Thorne,* I, chap. 18, pp. 297 ff.

which would increase rather than impair his already substantial fortune.[91] Nor did Ezekiel Brehgert have any compunction about risking his engagement to Georgiana by refusing her an expensive town house in London.[92]

The theme of middle-class indifference to aristocratic values was hardly Trollope's alone. One finds it also in Mrs. Gaskell's John Thornton, that apostle of "self-help" whose life ambition is "to hold and maintain a high, honourable place among the merchants of his country" and have "his word pass like gold."[93] Turn to Disraeli's *Coningsby* and one finds the same idea in Millbank's scorn of the aristocracy and pride in his factory as "a monument to the skill and power of his order."[94] But Trollope is rather more sensitive in delineating the compulsive acquisitiveness which this self-sufficiency sometimes involved, and it was precisely that aspect of the "new age" which so disconcerted Trollope himself. What troubled him was not trade or industry or money per se, but the apparently irresistible tendency of business to consume the entire lives of those whom it ensnared. Mr. Moffat's fault was not that he wanted to make money, but that he "had an eye to business in *everything.*"[95] Those two famous "commercial gentlemen," Mr. Kantwise and Mr. Moulder, go through life without stopping once to think or talk of anything but trade. Sir Roger Scatcherd is an even stronger portrait of this total preoccupation. Although he is a baronet, Scatcherd regards the honor merely as an accessory of great wealth, not a credential of gentility. If he has ambitions for a seat in Parliament, it is not to hobnob with aristocracy, but rather to sit there "as a great railway builder." Beyond that, the busi-

---

[91] *Ibid.,* chap. 17, p. 277, chap. 21, p. 353.

[92] *The Way We Live Now,* chap. 79, pp. 645 ff.

[93] Elizabeth Gaskell, *North and South* (New York: Putnam, 1906), chap. 10, p. 96, chap. 15, p. 133, chap. 20, p. 194, chap. 50, p. 500.

[94] New York: Knopf, 1937, bk. 4, chap. 3, p. 172, chap. 4, pp. 177–79.

[95] *Doctor Thorne,* I, chap. 14, p. 232.

ness of accumulating a fortune has left him no other object in
life except brandy. As he argues with Dr. Thorne,

And why should I not drink? . . . What gratification can I
have except the brandy bottle? . . . I'll tell you what,
Thorne, when a man has made three hundred thousand
pounds, there's nothing left for him but to die. It's all he's
good for then. When money's been made, the next thing is to
spend it. Now the man who makes it has not the heart to do
that.[96]

Although this is a clear warning that the surface self-
sufficiency of the middle class could mask more basic moral
and intellectual insufficiency, Trollope's very concern is a
reflection of the extent to which commercial-industrial values
had triumphed in England. In this sense, if one leaves aside
the dream of "finality" and Macaulay's view that universal
suffrage was "incompatible with civilization," there was obviously some significant, inherent social reality behind the
Whig theory of a "general class" whose interests were those
of society at large. If perhaps they were not quite the "natural
representatives of the human race," the members of the
middle class nevertheless composed an open, vital, burgeoning order—everything the French bourgeoisie was not. It is
scarcely surprising, then, that the *juste milieu* theory of the
middle class met rather different political fates in England
and France.

The July Regime: Aristotle Betrayed

In France, the middle-class mystique had practically no political currency outside the *juste milieu* itself. An Ultra like
Villèle clearly sensed the schizophrenia of the bourgeois soul
when, on the one hand, he described the middle class as "une

[96] *Ibid.,* chap. 10, pp. 173 ff.

aristocratie sans base réele," while on the other hand he explained his Restoration proposal to enlarge the electorate with the following rationale:

Since the beginning of the world, the last class has been under the influence of the first . . . and the middle class, envied by the last and the enemy of the first, composes the revolutionary party of society in all states. If you want the first class in your assembly, use the auxiliaries which it has within the last class, descend as low as you can and thus swamp the middle class which is the only enemy you have to fear.[97]

This not only repudiated the Doctrinaires' idea of a "general class," but it also shattered an assumption on which Aristotle had based his middle-class state: "There will be no fear that the rich will unite with the poor against the rulers. For neither of them will ever be willing to serve the other."[98]

On the opposite flank, Jules Michelet matched Villèle in his disdain for the bourgeoisie of the July Regime:

There was, at least, more consistency in the bourgeois of the former days. He admired himself in his privileges, sought to enlarge them, and looked upward. Our present bourgeois looks downward, sees the crowd mount behind him, as he has mounted, and does not like their aspiration; so recoils and fixes himself by the side of "the powers that be." Does he frankly confess his retrograde tendencies to himself? Rarely. His past life makes him shrink from it. He almost always remains in this contradictory position: liberal by principle, selfish by habit, wishing and not wishing.[99]

Even more moderate men of the left like Odilon Barrot and de Tocqueville shared this same view. After eighteen years of

[97] Villèle, *op. cit.*, I, 482, 489–90.

[98] *The Politics,* trans. Benjamin Jowett (New York: Modern Library, 1943), p. 194.

[99] Jules Michelet, *The People* (New York: Appleton, 1846), p. 89.

Louis Philippe and Guizot, de Tocqueville concluded that the middle-class spirit "in isolation can only produce a government without virtue or greatness."[100] Lamartine was even more blunt in his famous three-word verdict: "France is bored."

As one might expect, the objection of a moderate like de Tocqueville to the July Regime was that it embodied essentially the same attributes which we have seen in the bourgeoisie itself. Although it is not difficult to document that objection, one should first recognize that Guizot did bring a seeming stability to French government. The word "seeming" is important, however. After the precarious victory of 1830, the failure of the Doctrinaires to make a party was a lesson which Guizot never forgot. As he was to write in later years, his fixed purpose during the July Regime was the establishment of a government of men committed to the same ideas and supported in the Chamber by a faithful majority.[101] When he finally became master of the cabinet in 1840 after the long "movement-resistance" era of the '30s, Guizot proved remarkably successful in that purpose. Witness the eight-year longevity of his ministry. Although only an exhaustive narrative history[102] could detail the instances of parliamentary skill, royal support, and often, sheerly fortuitous circumstance which were involved in that success, two factors do deserve more than passing mention. These were the regime's use of administrative patronage within the Chamber and of governmental pressure in elections. For

[100] De Tocqueville, *Recollections,* trans. Alexander Teixeira de Mattos, ed. J. P. Mayer (Columbia University Press, 1949), pp. 3, 10–12. See also de Tocqueville's "Note sur la Classe Moyenne et le Peuple," *Études Économiques, Politiques et Littéraires* (Paris, 1866), pp. 514–19. For Odilon Barrot's attack on Guizot's view of the middle class, see the latter's *Histoire Parlementaire,* III, 102.

[101] *Mémoires,* VIII, 9–10; *Histoire Parlementaire,* V, 294.

[102] See Douglas Johnson, *op. cit.,* chaps. 4 and 5, for excellent recent account.

these techniques, "érigées en système"[103] under the late July Regime, not only suggest that sheer longevity is a false measure of the stability of Guizot's ministry; they also help explain why the political sympathy of society at large became increasingly alienated from the July Regime.

Although the Doctrinaires had on occasion scathingly denounced so-called administrative corruption before 1830,[104] the Chamber in 1846 included the impressive number of 184 "place men" who held office under a law which permitted a deputy to be also a public "fonctionnaire." The vast majority of these place men, around 145, formed a solid core of support for Guizot, many of them having obviously traded loyalty to the regime for lucrative magistracies and other jobs. That was a pattern of patronage for which E. L. Woodward has found an English parallel only in the House of Commons before the extensive reforms of the 1780s.[105] As for governmental influence in elections, the legends of bribery and other blatant forms of electoral chicanery which have always been associated with the July Regime may well be less than just. Nevertheless it seems fair to suggest that the still relatively manageable size of the Regime's electorate (one-fourth that of England's after 1832) and the centralized *préfet* system probably did give the government a significant advantage. Even Douglas Johnson, who has recently taken some pains to try to discredit the legends of corruption, confesses that some degree of administrative influence in elections must have been necessary to maintain Guizot. Johnson also raises the more fundamental question of whether the

[103] Paul Bastid, *Les Institutions Politiques de la Monarchie Parlementaire Française (1814–48)* (Paris: Éditions du Recueil Sirey, 1954), pp. 234–35.

[104] See, for example, Royer-Collard's criticism of Villèle in Barante, *op. cit.,* II, 228.

[105] E. L. Woodward, *French Revolutions* (Oxford, 1930), p. 130. For effect of English reforms, see B. Kemp, *King and Commons, 1660–1832* (London: Macmillan, 1957), pp. 95–110; and N. Gash, *Politics in the Age of Peel,* p. 346.

July Regime's centralized administrative system was really compatible with representative government. He suggests that it was, provided one defines representative government, à la Guizot of the late July Regime, in terms of maintaining a solid majority for the party in power.[106] But that observation itself seems to imply an incompatibility if one defines representative government in terms of giving a parliamentary minority the opportunity to become a majority. Thus I think it is not unreasonable to conclude that governmental pressure and patronage probably did help save Guizot in the 1842 elections and helped give him a considerable victory in 1846. As we shall see in a moment, however, these techniques probably also contributed to his final undoing in 1848.

   With both parliament and the electorate fairly well in hand, it seemed to Guizot that the great question of the last half-century had finally been answered affirmatively: "whether the ideas of 1789 and the social state to which they had led could ever yield a stable and regular government."[107] For the bourgeois monarchy he set a stolidly bourgeois goal: "That France prosper, that she live with freedom, wealth, intelligence, and without trouble."[108]

   But trouble there was. After all, Guizot's Chamber and *pays légal* were not France. And outside those two *juste milieu* bastions, the left began to wield the initiative. As this happened, the very techniques with which Guizot had "consolidated" his government proved something of a trap for him. For one thing, those techniques increased demands for reform by encouraging the prevalent idea that Guizot's

[106] Johnson, *op. cit.,* pp. 223 ff. See also Peter Campbell, *French Electoral Systems and Elections, 1789–1957* (London: Faber and Faber, 1958), pp. 33, 61–63; and Sherman Kent, *Electoral Procedures under Louis Philippe* (Yale University Press, 1937), pp. 106 ff. Stendhal has a marvelous description of a *juste milieu* election in *Lucien Leuwen, Book Two, The Telegraph,* pp. 145–242.
[107] *Histoire Parlementaire,* III, 153; *Mémoires,* VI, 377.
[108] Quoted in Bastid, *op. cit.,* p. 133.

regime was riddled with corruption. For another thing, thanks to the system of place men and electoral influence, the Chamber's moderate, dynastic opposition, led by such men as Odilon Barrot, Duvergier de Hauranne, and de Tocqueville, began to feel permanently excluded from power. This obviously made the "chain of friendship" on the left all the more dangerous, for their only alternative was to seek or accept support outside both parliament and the electorate. When voting and debating within the *juste milieu* arena proved futile, that alternative became almost irresistible and Guizot's position perilous.

On the moderates' left, the Republicans had since 1830 begun to make up for their relative weakness during the Restoration. They now gathered in the strengthened sections of the "Société des Droits de l'Homme" and deluged the *juste milieu* with propaganda through a highly effective press. In the *National,* Armand Carrel demanded a republic with moderate extension of the franchise; in a variety of other journals a chorus of Godefroy Cavaignac, Ledru-Rollin, Garnier-Pagès, Dupont de l'Eure, and Louis Blanc all insisted on nothing less than popular sovereignty and universal suffrage.[109] Moreover, as the name Blanc suggests, the horror of all this for the *juste milieu* was that the left was no longer merely Republican. The socialism to which Guizot had always insisted universal suffrage would lead was now added to Jacobinism. "The Social Republic . . . odious and impossible . . . the most perverse of all chimeras" was the new menace which divided "workmen . . . against their master, or the people against the middle classes." "Chaos is now concealed under one word — Democracy."[110] The writings of Étienne Cabet, the Abbé de Lamennais, Pierre-Joseph Proud-

[109] Paul Thureau-Dangin, *Histoire de la Monarchie de Juillet* (Paris: 1887–92), I, 571–94, and II, 213–20; G. Weill, *Histoire du Parti Républicain en France* (Paris, 1928), pp. 74–137; Blanc, *op. cit.,* I, 573–76.

[110] *Democracy in France,* pp. 10, 36, 57.

hon and Blanc announced the new menace. In turn, "chaos" became reality for the *juste milieu* with the Paris strikes of 1832–33, the 1831 and 1834 insurrections at Lyons, Giuseppe Fieschi's attempt on the King, and Louis Auguste Blanqui's "Society of Seasons" disturbance in 1839. To all this the *juste milieu*'s response was precisely what "chaos" deserved: the brute repression exemplified by Soult's army at Lyons and the notorious Rue Transnonian massacre in Paris in 1834.[111]

Although such measures had seemingly checked the challenge from the left by the time Guizot came to power in 1840, that impression was illusory. For such measures failed to reach basic sources of discontent on which the left continued to feed. One such source was the class structure which we have already noted in French society. Another and related source was the economic and social distress of incipient industrialism: sweat shop wages, the illegality of unions, crowded and unsanitary urban living conditions, acute unemployment in three serious depressions between 1830 and 1847, and lastly, the psychological trauma which any society suffers in transition from the rhythm of peasant-handicraft life to the discipline of the machine-factory system.[112] But if Guizot may have sensed that the "social problem" lay behind the menace on the left, his response was to declare complacently, "all the great conquests are made, all the great interests are satisfied."[113] If he recognized that some human misery remained, Guizot's view of man was apparently still what it had been in the *History of Civilization:* "His faults affect me more than his suffering."[114] In any event, it was only a

[111] For survey of the rise of socialist agitation, see especially E. Levasseur, *Histoire des Classes Ouvrières et de l'Industrie en France de 1789 à 1870* (Paris, 1904), II, 3–66.

[112] *Ibid.*, pp. 259–64; A. L. Dunham, *La Révolution Industrielle en France, 1815–48* (Paris: Librairie Marcel Rivière et Cie, 1953), pp. 169–73.

[113] *Histoire Parlementaire*, III, 564.

[114] *History of Civilization in Europe*, p. 236.

"philanthropic dream" to suppose that the government could or should alleviate suffering by concerning itself with "the relations between property and labor." Although extraordinary circumstances might occasionally justify an exception, any attempt by government to interfere was in general both "chimerical and disastrous."[115]

One alternative was left. The common focus of all opposition to the July Regime was the demand for a more liberal franchise. Although a strategic retreat on this issue might have saved him, Guizot was still adamant. Universal suffrage of course remained beyond consideration. Continuing the equation between property and intelligence, he granted that as the "capacities" of citizens expanded, so would the electorate. But this implied no need to tamper with the "perfection" of the middle-class franchise or even with the system of place men in the Chamber. Almost until the last minute of his regime, when it was then too late, Guizot refused even an investigation of the regime's patronage in the Chamber. As for enlarging the electorate, he dismissed out of hand Duvergier de Hauranne's moderate proposal for a uniform 100-franc franchise. And even though the 200-franc electoral law of 1831 had provided a special franchise for members of the Institute of France and retired military officers paying only 100 francs in direct taxation, Guizot also treated with disdain the idea of broadening out those narrow exceptions to include, in general, all educated professional classes. "The difference is great between political capacity and purely intellectual capacity." Excessive faith in the latter has been the "malady of our age." Intelligence can yield political capacity only when "enlightened by social situation"—by a stake in the "true and essential interests of the social order."[116]

In his stubbornness Guizot badly misjudged the demand for moderate electoral reform by considering it as somehow

[115] *Histoire Parlementaire*, I, 325–28, and II, 225.   [116] *Ibid.*, V, 385–86.

the handiwork of that same Jacobin-Socialist left which held such a peculiar facility of terror over the *juste milieu*. He failed to see the demand as a deeply felt symbol of discontent throughout the nation in general. He believed that modern society, "occupied with its own domestic interests," really did not aspire "to govern itself." Electoral reform had no "serious motive" behind it. It was simply a false, superficial movement, improvised by the extremists and exploited by the moderate left as a matter of parliamentary tactics.[117]

Yet Guizot's even more monumental mistake was not to realize that moderate reform would have probably meant a victory, rather than a retreat, for "middle-class" government. For the irony was that even the 200-franc franchise of 1831 barred from the electorate large and conservative groups seemingly included in Guizot's vague definitions of the class: not only many professions, but also the bulk of the "petite bourgeoisie" and small landowners.[118] Admitted to the electorate, these would have added strength and stability to the *juste milieu;* excluded they could only imperil it. To the end Guizot denied that he had set any "narrow limits" to the middle class.[119] But deeds do speak louder than words. With the artificial construct of the July Regime's *pays légal,* he betrayed broad sectors of French society which had clearly been included a generation earlier in the concept of the *tier état.* He instead narrowly identified as the middle class what could only be described as the "grande bourgeoisie."

In so doing he himself surely revealed something of that same schizophrenia which we have already seen in the French bourgeoisie itself. For if Guizot often talked of "social equality" in defending the middle class, he apparently also saw the class as that "veritable and legitimate aristoc-

[117] *Ibid.,* I, 316; III, 556–57, 562–66; and V, 381–82.
[118] This has of course often been noted. See Faguet, *op. cit.,* p. 341; Woodward, *Three Studies in European Conservatism,* p. 225.
[119] *Mémoires,* VIII, 522–23; *Histoire Parlementaire,* III, 104, 555–56.

racy" which it was the job of government to draw from society.[120] There is perhaps another sense as well in which Guizot's response significantly reflected the disintegration of French society. If the Great Revolution was a prime source of the *juste milieu*'s terror of the left, surely the lack of effective communication within society and, in particular, the bourgeoisie's isolation from the rest of society must have added a certain element of unreality, even hysteria, to *juste milieu* calculations of danger. Thus Guizot's regime hardly embodied the Aristotelian virtues of "reason" and "moderation." Instead it demonstrated narrow self-interest, stubbornness, fear, and paralysis—all the weaknesses of the bourgeoisie itself.

One might also suggest that in the end the strategist of siege succumbed to the psychology of siege. Guizot had fought so laboriously against the Ultras during the Restoration that he instinctively resisted as illegitimate whatever new demands he met on his other flank. He had seen the Doctrinaires and himself compromise their tenets more than once in order to wrest the initiative from the right. In 1830 he had even seen them become involved in a revolution which might easily have been disastrous for the *juste milieu*. So determined was he to avoid still another revolution, that he somehow equated concession with revolution. The way to hold the *juste milieu* was simply not to give ground. The psychology of siege had blinded him to the movement of French politics from right to left. He failed to see that his own resistance was forging on the left the last links in that chain of friendship, from Barrot to Ledru-Rollin to Blanc, which would open the floodgates of revolution in 1848. He failed to see that the true *juste milieu*, the only ground which could be held, was now on his left. The final irony was that the *juste milieu* did not deserve the distinction of being either "middle class" or "the middle"!

[120] *History of Representative Government*, p. 66.

Chartism: Treason Thwarted

In England the theory of the middle class fared quite differently in terms of the political currency which it had to the left of the *juste milieu*. Francis Place, for example, may on occasion have said some unkind words about the "shopkeeping race," but he himself had risen from poverty to be quite a prosperous shopkeeper and he often parrotted the Whig description of the middle class as the true locus of "talent, honesty, and businesslike habits."[121] Although Attwood's belief in a managed nongold standard monetary policy was a departure from laissez faire economics, his scheme assumed throughout an identity of interest between the middle and respectable working classes.[122] Even Macaulay's archantagonist, James Mill, ended his *Essay on Government* with a eulogy of the Whigs' chosen class:

The opinions of that class of the people who are below the middle rank are formed, and their minds directed, by that intelligent, that virtuous rank, who come the most immediately in contact with them . . . to whom their children look up as models for their imitation, whose opinions they hear daily repeated, and account it their honor to adopt. There can be no doubt that the middle rank, which gives to science, to art, and to legislation their most distinguished ornaments, and is the chief source of all that has exalted and refined human nature, is that portion of the community, of which, if the basis of representation were ever so far extended, the opinion would ultimately decide. Of the people beneath

[121] Quoted in Wallas, *op. cit.,* pp. 155, 266.
[122] Asa Briggs, "Social Structure and Politics in Birmingham and Lyons," *British Journal of Sociology,* I (March 1950), 71–73; G. D. H. Cole, *Chartist Portraits* (London: Macmillan, 1941), pp. 113, 118.

them, a vast majority would be sure to be guided by their advice and example.[123]

Although Macaulay claimed that this admission of an identity of interests between classes undercut the *Essay*'s entire argument in favor of a franchise which would be close to universal, one can argue conversely that Mill's statement of lower-class deference to the leadership and values of the middle class actually tended to support the extension of the franchise to *both* classes.[124] In any event the passage is clearly a more sanguine view of the middle class than one finds on the moderate French left and reflects Mill's commitment to that class' commercial-industrial values.

The importance of this is immediately apparent in the moderate Radicals' response to Chartism, the most serious challenge which the English *juste milieu* faced between the birth pangs of 1832 and the transition of 1867. In every sense Chartism was an attack on the terms of 1832. It was an attack not only on the surviving rotten boroughs, the continuing influence of aristocracy, and the Whig insistence on "finality," but, more fundamentally, on the middle class and its values per se. Like the movement for radical political reform in France, the Chartist demand for universal suffrage, the ballot, equal electoral districts, and annual parliaments was largely the surface expression of far deeper social distresses caused by the industrial revolution. But unlike the French demand, Chartism ended in an almost pathetic fizzle. It was once again the extreme left, not the moderate center, which found itself isolated and impotent.

[123] From James Mill: *An Essay on Government* (pp. 90–91) edited by Currin V. Shields, copyright, 1955, by The Liberal Arts Press, Inc., reprinted by permission of the Liberal Arts Press Division of The Bobbs-Merrill Company, Inc.

[124] See Joseph Hamburger, "James Mill on Universal Suffrage and the Middle Class," *Journal of Politics,* XXIV (Feb. 1962), 167 ff., for an argument to this effect and other comments on Mill's celebrated eulogy of the class.

In the beginning, however, this pattern was hardly clear. It seemed at the outset that Chartism might secure the support and leadership of those moderate Radicals who had stood with the Whigs in 1832, but by the late 30s appeared ready to reopen the issue of political reform. For example, in 1837–38, Place helped William Lovett draft the original Charter and smiled on the leaders of the emerging movement. But significantly, Place tendered his services only on condition that the Chartist leaders promise to prevent any speeches in favor of socialism from their platforms. Similarly, Attwood revived his Birmingham Union in 1837 to support the Chartist demands and his currency scheme.[125] Even the *Westminster Review,* now over its entrancement with the Whigs, seemed to play into the hands of the Chartists. As in the 20s, the *Review* was again sneering at the Whigs as a mere "coterie" and calling class representation "the master fallacy of all."[126] New economic reforms were now impossible without "further Parliamentary reform" in order to change the "vicious constitution of the legislature."[127] Although the moderate Radicals had household rather than universal suffrage in mind, they were certain that Whig fears of "mischievous opinions and feelings" among the working classes were "vastly exaggerated." The London Chartist leaders, for example, were "not only some of the best men, but . . . also, to a great extent, instructed and cultivated men."[128]

This trust proved to be badly misplaced. It soon became clear that political reform for the Chartists was only a stepping stone to ends which the Place-Attwood-*Westminster*

---

[125] Wallas, *op. cit.,* pp. 359 ff.; Mark Hovell, *The Chartist Movement* (Manchester University Press, 1925), pp. 99 ff.

[126] XXV (July 1836), 281; *London Review,* I (April–July 1835), 369 (incorporated as Vol. XXX of the *Westminster Review*).

[127] *Westminster Review,* XXXII (April 1839), 476, 484–85.

[128] *London Review,* I (April–July 1835), 357 (incorporated as Vol. XXX of the *Westminster Review*); *Westminster Review,* XXXII (April 1839), 497.

Review moderates would surely regard as "mischievous."
Even the London leaders like William Lovett, who pledged
to use "moral" rather than "physical" force, accepted the
principles of Robert Owen.[129] The *Northern Star,* the movement's chief organ, was explicit in declaring, "Socialism and
Chartism pursue the same ends."[130] And Joseph Stephens,
speaking to a mass meeting at Manchester, defined universal
suffrage not in political terms, but in those of the working
man's guaranteed right to decent shelter, work, wages, and
hours.[131] Added to this socialist strain was an almost neofeudal
rejection of industrialism by the leaders, who, after 1842,
gained control of Chartism. Feargus O'Connor, for example,
fulminated throughout his career against "machinery" as the
"great monster enemy" responsible for all economic distress.
He insisted that peasant proprietorship was "the best basis of
society" and in 1845 tried to revitalize Chartism with a coop-
erative scheme to buy up small plots of land on which industrial working men were to be relocated.[132]

As soon as this socialist, anti-industrial bias of Chartism
became obvious, it lost the sympathy and potential leadership
of the moderate Radicals who had access to the vital center of
English politics. To return to the old metaphor, the possibility of a "chain of friendship" between extreme and moderate
Radicalism was broken, and the original chain between the
moderates and the *juste milieu* was reestablished. As early as
1839 Attwood realized that Chartism could not be reconciled
with his own middle-class attachments, and he bowed out of
further agitation, "exhausted, disappointed and ailing."[133]
Place also soon became disillusioned not only with the socialism, but also the strikes and widespread disorders of Chart-

[129] M. Beer, *British Socialism* (London: Allen & Unwin, 1953), II, 46 ff.
[130] Quoted *ibid.,* p. 45.
[131] *Ibid.,* pp. 47–48.
[132] Hovell, *op. cit.,* pp. 216, 306; M. Beer, *op. cit.,* II, 59, 155–56 (italics
mine).
[133] *Ibid.,* p. 81.

ism. By 1840 he had concluded, "There is at present no possibility of doing good to the working people or to anybody else by any proposal for reform in Parliament. The working people are not in a condition to join in any scheme of the sort, neither will they be so for some time to come."[134]

After the Chartist mass marches and violence of August 1842, the *Westminster Review* also suddenly became anxious to avoid the very political reform it had earlier urged. Granted that the economic distress of which the Chartists complained was real, they were attributing it to causes with which it had "no connexion" and asking "as remedies what could only operate as aggravations." In the hands of such "uneducated people," the self-government demanded by the Chartists would "assuredly prove a curse as fearful as any with which God, in his anger, has ever visited his creatures." If the working classes really wished to elevate themselves, they would abandon both radical political reform and socialism in favor of *"some object which the middle classes will join them in demanding."* What would that be? Quite simply, more education and repeal of the Corn Laws, which caused economic distress by shackling industrial growth. Give the nation these reforms, "and organic changes will cease to be demanded."[135]

Although one could hardly give sole credit to Place, Attwood, and the *Westminster Review* for the failure of Chartism, they were not proved false prophets. If Feargus O'Connor had returned to England starry-eyed from the revolutions on the Continent, he was a pale, frightened man when he met the Chartist gathering in London in April 1848, told them to go home, and gladly permitted Chartism's last petition to be innocuously delivered in three cabs to the House of Commons. There it was received not with fear, but with

[134] Wallas, *op. cit.,* pp. 388–91.
[135] XXXVIII (Oct. 1842), 397, 407–8, 412–13.

laughter. Eight years before, Disraeli had advised the Chartists that in England "even treason, to be successful, must be patrician."[136] But perhaps the *Westminster Review*'s suggestion that it must be "middle class" was even more to the point. The sense of this will become doubly clear when we come to the messianic success of the "free trade" crusade and the strange fall from grace of Lord Henry Peter Brougham.

[136] Quoted by W. F. Monypenny, *Life of Disraeli* (New York: Macmillan, 1912), II, 87.

Chapter Four

FREEDOM THROUGH HISTORY?

THE Great Revolution made freedom forever after an unavoidable concept of political theory in both France and England. That meant that any nineteenth-century regime or school of thought which set class limits to the franchise was well advised to offer some meaningful form of freedom *outside* the realm of political participation. Whether the middle-class theory of representation had currency beyond the chosen order or not, the Doctrinaires and Whigs were only prudent to hold out some further conciliatory substitute for political democracy. To do so was not an insurmountable challenge. The militant creed of civil liberty which Benjamin Constant combined with a property-based franchise, the millennial economic freedom which the Corn Law crusade promised, and Marx's grounding of freedom in the inexorable march of history can all be considered, in varying degrees, successful responses to the problem.

Resistance and Protection

The response of the French *juste milieu,* however, cannot be considered successful—in either the civil, economic, or historical realm. Although the Doctrinaires' theory of freedom reflected underlying political reality more accurately than their concepts of sovereignty and representation, that fact did not make the theory viable, any more than the Charter's reflection of the contradictory principles of the Revolution and Ancien Regime gave it promise of enduring.

In defining freedom the Doctrinaires seemed to qualify the assumption that the components of the mixed state and the diverse interests of society would somehow always harmonize in sweet reasonableness. Even when divided, power must remain subject to "suspicion" and must "continue to legitimize itself."[1] If diverse interests do not harmonize, their conflict can itself be a protection against the tyranny of any one interest. The "laborous" search for reason, said Guizot, is advanced, not defeated, by "obstacle and combat."[2] Hence Royer-Collard defined liberties as *"resistances"* which are "not less necessary to legitimacy than it is to liberties."[3] Both theorists postulated freedom of the press as a necessary condition of legitimate government and the cornerstone of all other liberties.[4] Without it France would return to servitude. "Publicity watches over the powers; enlightens them, warns them, reprimands them, resists them. . . . *It is . . . a necessity. That word carries with it its own force."*[5] The other civil liberties were defended with the same rationale. For example, Royer-Collard called trial by jury "also a liberty—I mean by that any limitation of established power."[6] The irremovability of magistrates was a guarantee of judicial independence against intimidation by the state.[7] Freedom of religion not only recognized a spiritual realm beyond the jurisdiction of the state, but also prevented the Church from becoming a prop for an absolutist state.[8]

Freedom as a "necessary resistance" to power has, however,

---

[1] Guizot, *History of Representative Government*, p. 73.

[2] Quoted by Pouthas, *op. cit.,* p. 321, from Guizot's unpublished "Philosophie Politique."   [3] Barante, *op. cit.,* II, 115 (italics mine).

[4] Guizot, *History of Representative Government*, pp. 77, 265, 348; Barante, *op. cit.,* I, 340.

[5] *Ibid.,* II, 133 (italics mine).   [6] Nesmes-Desmarets, *op. cit.,* p. 252.

[7] Barante, *op. cit.,* I, 165 ff.   [8] *Ibid.,* II, 99 ff.

both philosophic and strategic implications. It is true that the Doctrinaires were often eloquent defenders of civil liberty and insisted that, unlike political liberty, it belonged to man simply "by the fact that he is man."[9] But I would argue that it is difficult to sustain an interpretation, such as Laski's, that Royer-Collard grounded liberty in a Kantian conception of human personality.[10] For Royer-Collard's few scattered references to man's "dignity" or "natural right,"[11] there are dozens more to "necessity."[12] And the crucial point is that his "necessity" was in large measure *external* to the individual. Instead of emphasizing freedom as the necessary condition of individual dignity and self-fulfillment, he emphasized freedom as the necessary condition of a stable social and political order. Freedom was necessary because any unchecked abuse of power threatened to become despotism, and despotism in turn threatened the disintegration of the existing order in revolution. In France, Guizot observed, "every storm becomes a flood."[13] Doctrinaire "necessity" thus meant a primary concern not with the individual himself, but rather with society at large. To put the point somewhat differently, the liberties of the Revolution were really reduced to positional or strategic safeguards for the *juste milieu* against the extremes of right and left. And I think that anyone must confess that freedom defined in those terms is essentially a negative category. Once again, bourgeois "individualism" is compromised. But this time one need not look to political and social reality to find the compromise; it is clear on the face of Doctrinaire theory itself.

This point becomes even more explicit if one compares the Doctrinaire statement of liberty with that of Benjamin Constant. Although usually and justly ranged to the left of the

---

[9] See above, p. 57. [10] Laski, *op. cit.*, pp. 301, 310–11.

[11] Barante, *op. cit.*, I, 171; II, 293.

[12] *Ibid.*, I, 165 ff.; II, 99–103, 129–44, 290–312. [13] *Mémoires*, II, 4.

Doctrinaires, Constant shared their limited approval of the Revolution, their defense of a restricted franchise, and rejection of individual will as the basis of representation.[14] What really distinguishes him from the *juste milieu* is the radical individualism of his concept of liberty. For if Constant also postulated individual liberty as a limit on sovereignty, he refused to ground it in political or social "necessity."[15] Liberty had, for him, an independent validity of its own. "Citizens possess individual rights which are independent of all social or political authority."[16] "The jurisdiction of . . . sovereignty stops at the point at which the independence and existence of the individual begins."[17] "By liberty, I mean the triumph of individuality"—"in religion, in philosophy, in literature, in industry, in politics."[18] This is clearly a preoccupation with the individual and his self-fulfillment that the Doctrinaire theory of liberty lacks.

Grounded in "necessity," Doctrinaire freedom often proved to have a curious content. For if necessity itself meant the strategic requirements for holding the middle ground against the extremes, those requirements in *juste milieu* France often dictated compromises quite at odds with the meaning which freedom has when it is grounded exclusively in individual right. For example, the Doctrinaires found one freedom which it was necessary *not* to embrace— the freedom of individuals, groups, and local authorities in the field of education. Why? The answer is that they saw another more immediate and important consideration: preventing the Ultras from using such freedom to reestablish the clergy's old monopoly of education. Hence, the Doctrinaires, again in contrast with Benjamin Constant who apparently

---

[14] Benjamin Constant, *Cours de Politique* (Paris, 1872), I, 12, 54, 98. See also Burdeau, *op. cit.,* pp. 130, 134–36, 409, 418.

[15] Constant, *op. cit.,* I, 348.   [16] *Ibid.,* p. 13.   [17] *Ibid.,* p. 9.

[18] Constant, "Mélanges de Littérature et de Politique," *Oeuvres* (Lyon: Bibliothèque de la Pléiade, 1957), p. 835.

was ready to take that risk, defended the state's overarching control of all French education. On one occasion Royer-Collard even commented: "The University has a monopoly in education, in almost the same sense that the courts have a monopoly in dispensing justice, or the army in public force."[19] If Royer-Collard and Guizot also questioned on more than one occasion the strictness and centralization of state control, that should not hide the fact that in general they took a very skeptical attitude toward freedom in education.[20]

Toward education itself, however, they took a quite different attitude. Indeed, the keen and continuing interest of the Doctrinaires in education—from the 1814 plan for seventeen regional universities to Guizot's 1833 law establishing a public primary school in every commune—is itself a revealing aspect of the *juste milieu*. Always the Doctrinaires emphasized the importance of national education in unifying French society around the great moral and political values on which (they believed) the state was based. This was precisely the rationale which Charles Renouvier, Jules Ferry, and the republicans of the Third Republic were to express a half-century later. The pattern is the same. Besieged from right and left, the center seeks to convert its enemies with education. But the hope of converting enemies suggests a certain faith that one's own values are universals. If the "necessary freedoms" of Royer-Collard seem not to have been grounded in the sanctity of human personality, his exclusion of education from the category of liberty seems, at the same time, to imply a belief in the underlying moral solidarity of mankind. That premise was to be explicit in Renouvier.[21] For both the

[19] Nesmes-Desmarets, *op. cit.*, p. 286.
[20] See Johnson, *op. cit.*, pp. 88 ff., for survey of Guizot's interest and work in education.
[21] See discussion in Michel, *op. cit.*, pp. 595 ff.; and Soltau, *op. cit.*, pp. 306 ff.

juste milieu and Third Republic, education thus seemed to promise an expanding center, rather than mere resistance against the rest of society. Yet in this apparent escape from a purely defensive posture, the Doctrinaires and later republicans succumbed to that same unreality which we have found in the sovereignty of reason and the middle-class mystique. In the nature of things, education could hardly be the magic catalyst of French society. Men proved far more preoccupied with what divided them than with what they might have in common.

To return to the "necessary freedoms," even the much heralded freedom of the press did not escape compromise by the men of the *juste milieu* in the face of what they considered its abuse by the extremes of left and right. After all, how does one distinguish between an abuse of freedom and an abuse of power, especially when both threaten what the Doctrinaires feared most: the disintegration of the social order? And when free speech so threatened, necessity demanded that the Doctrinaires curtail that freedom, just as they had freedom of education. For example, the "September Laws" of 1835 responded to the onslaughts of the leftist press and Fieschi's attempt on the King's life by increasing the "caution money" required of Paris papers to 100,000 francs, and by imposing a 50,000-franc fine for any expression which could be interpreted as "an affront to the King" or as "arousing hatred or contempt of the government." Those two catch-all categories accounted for at least a third of the formidable number of press prosecutions under the July Regime. A prison term so often accompanied the fine that the editors of the *Tribune* and *National* had special quarters at Sainte-Pélagie.[22]

Although Royer-Collard came out of political retirement

[22] Irene Collins, *The Government and the Newspaper Press in France, 1814–1881* (Oxford University Press, 1959), pp. 82 ff.

to protest the severity of these particular restrictions,[23] he himself had more than once joined in the compromise of press rights when he was still an active strategist of "necessity" during the Restoration. Even if he invariably expressed reluctance in yielding to restriction and often conditioned it with such safeguards as a one-year limit or jury trial of offenses, the points yielded nevertheless impaired the integrity of Doctrinaire liberty. For example, in 1818 during the moderates' struggle against a virulent Ultra press, Royer-Collard approved a measure to punish both direct and indirect provocations against the government. "A government which has protection against only direct provocation stands exposed without defense to the most piercing and formidable shafts from the press."[24] On another occasion, in supporting a center ministry against the left, he argued with disconcerting ease that restrictions on the establishment of journals could be defended without reference to the freedom to publish "opinions." If the latter freedom was protected by the Charter, the former was merely "a speculation, both political and commercial."[25] Thus did *juste milieu* civil liberty suffer at the hands of necessity. Freedom was not only tolerable, but necessary, so long as it remained a positional weapon with which the middle ground could be held against the extremes. As soon, however, as freedom threatened to become a weapon which the extremes could wield effectively against the *juste milieu,* the Doctrinaires developed second thoughts which tarnished their initially eloquent theoretical defense of civil liberty.

The inadequacy of Doctrinaire freedom is equally evident in the economic realm. The response which we have seen Guizot make to the "social problem" was obviously not designed to warm men's hearts.[26] Heartlessness, however, is not necessarily fatal in politics, if it can be masked or rationalized

[23] Barante, *op. cit.,* II, 505.   [24] *Ibid.,* I, 344.
[25] *Ibid.,* pp. 482–83.   [26] See above, pp. 91–92.

in messianic terms. In that sense, the *juste milieu*'s deeper failure was not to find a viable issue, comparable to English "free trade," which could translate the raw facts of laissez faire into a millennial creed of reform. From first to last Guizot had *only* the cruel side of laissez faire to offer. He had no Cobdenesque utopia of cheap bread and world peace to hold out as a palliative to human suffering. True, it would not be fair to blame the Doctrinaires alone for this failure. As Frederic Bastiat found, the cause of free trade could meet with only scant success in the France of the 1840s, and it is doubtful indeed that France could have withstood open competition with England.[27] The backwardness of French industry reflected, in turn, the continuing ambivalence to commercial-industrial values which we have already observed in society at large. It should not be surprising, then, that just as the narrow limits which Guizot set to the electorate revealed the schizophrenia of the bourgeois soul, so also did his view of laissez faire.

His defense of the protectionism of the July Regime is a case in point. If, as we will see, Macaulay could compensate for a laissez faire attitude toward working-class distress by attacking the "wicked Corn Law interests" and joining Cobden's promise of peaceful abundance, Guizot could not. On the one hand he preached that government interference to alleviate the social problem would be "disastrous," while on

---

[27] See discussion in Dunham, *op. cit.*, pp. 348–58; and Levasseur, *op. cit.*, II, 68–92. French tariffs probably were higher than necessary, but moderate reduction could never have had the millennial appeal that total repeal had in England. In the early 1840s the July Regime did conclude a number of commercial agreements with neighboring countries. However, these agreements met considerable resistance within France, seemed to disadvantage as often as they helped French interests, and were never extended to include England. At Bordeaux in 1846, Bastiat and other liberal economists formed an "Association pour la liberté des échanges," modeled on the Anti-Corn Law League, but hardly matching the League in results. See John Morley's *Life of Cobden* (New York: Macmillan, n.d.), I, 421, for Cobden's failure to interest Louis Philippe in the subject of free trade.

the other hand he insisted that "all responsible governments" should protect "established interests" from the "vicissitudes of unlimited foreign competition."[28] Although he later seemingly approved of England's repeal of the Corn Laws, given England's circumstances, he declared: "No one, gentlemen, is more a friend than I am of the influence of landed property, I say of the preponderance of the agricultural interest within a great country; I am convinced that it is on this interest that the prosperity and the security of the social state rest."[29] England itself owed "its force, its liberty, its prosperity" in large measure to landed property, and Guizot was certain that Peel could have no intention of ending the "ascendancy" of that interest.[30]

This almost Southeyesque glorification of land in place of commerce and industry was an incongruous but recurring theme with the archtheorist of the middle class. Writing in 1849 to his Tory friend, John Wilson Croker, Guizot again praised the wisdom of French cereal tariffs and declared the landed influence "the very foundation of society, the source of its grandeur, security, morality, and force." In *Democracy in France* he wrote glowingly of the small manufacturer or tradesman who invested in and retired to land. For "property in land is more consonant than any other to the nature of man . . . to his moral development." If trade was virtually the handmaiden of morality for Cobden and Macaulay, not for Guizot. It might develop a man's skill and wit, but only land could keep him "constantly in the presence of God."[31]

God might well agree with Guizot, but this theme could not give Doctrinaire freedom the *élan* necessary to make the *juste milieu* a vital center. As we have seen, ambivalence to commercial-industrial values, however widespread, was *not* an agent of social integration, but quite the opposite. When

---

[28] *Histoire Parlementaire*, IV, 544.   [29] *Ibid.*, V, 117.
[30] *Ibid.*, p. 118.
[31] *The Croker Papers*, II, 391–92; *Democracy in France*, pp. 43–45.

he turned to the realm of economic freedom, Guizot thus compromised for the second time the dream of a middle class which would universalize itself. First, he had equated that class with what was actually "la grande bourgeoisie." Second, he unmistakably revealed his own suspicion of the very values which were the currency of social mobility. The price he paid was to have the world realize that *juste milieu* economic freedom meant neither more nor less than indifference to the social problem. That hardly promised to reconcile the middle and lower classes, or distract the latter from mischievous designs of their own.[32]

Guizot on History

Guizot, however, remained more an optimist than a pessimist. If his optimism did not reflect his own political fate, it did reflect his study of the broad sweep of history. The belief in progress for which he is always remembered suggests that Doctrinaire theory, in a sense, offered a concept of history as a substitute for the tangible freedom which the *juste milieu* failed to provide in the here and now. That is a strategy

[32] It has sometimes been argued that a more adventurous foreign policy might have achieved this purpose, since the glory of France has often proved a standard to which all Frenchmen are ready to rally. Athough I have not dealt with foreign policy in this study of *juste milieu* middlingness, perhaps it is appropriate to remark here that that omission does not weaken my analysis. For one thing, the deeply fragmentized nature of French society and politics suggests that a more aggressive foreign policy could have been only a temporary prop to the July Regime. For another thing, such a policy might well have brought Guizot's fall all the more quickly. Guizot himself saw the specter of internal revolution behind the demand for foreign adventures and claimed that any policy which unsettled the post-1815 settlement in Europe would threaten the *juste milieu* settlement in France. Whether that was an accurate calculation or not, it simply underlines the strategic and psychological implications of the *juste milieu* position. For discussion of July Regime foreign policy, see Johnson, *op. cit.,* pp. 263 ff.

which has seldom worked in the real world of politics. Although one might argue that the Marxists have been successful with it, Guizot was not. Nevertheless, his view of history is an interesting final response of Doctrinaire thought to the inescapable category of freedom.

For Guizot the ideas of "civilization" and "progress" were virtually synonymous: "the first idea comprised in the word civilization . . . is the notion of progress, of development. It calls up within us the notion of a people advancing, of a people in a course of improvement and amelioration."[33] His favorite theme was to describe the majestic rise of European civilization since the Roman Empire, and to assure his readers that progress would carry on indefinitely into the future. "All Europe, and notably France, has marched for fifteen centuries along the same path of liberty and general progress."[34] Modern France now enjoyed "a degree of justice, well-being, and security" which no other age had even conceived possible.[35] Ultimately the "law of nature" which decreed progress in history would bring even the end of war. For "the empire of morality . . . is truly advancing . . . considerations of right and of public welfare exercise far more influence than ever before over questions of war and peace."[36] Men may still take up arms, but even with the first steps they already hesitate, embarrassed and uncertain to find themselves at odds with the "real needs, the profound instincts of modern societies."[37]

Guizot's approach to history was not, however, as simple as these rather naive statements of faith suggest. Indeed, his critics have sometimes been misled on this score. J. B. Bury, for example, finds in Guizot's theme of progress "the most important positive idea of 18th century speculation, standing forth *detached and independent, no longer bound to a sys-*

[33] *History of Civilization in Europe*, p. 22.
[34] *Histoire Parlementaire*, I, cxl.   [35] *Mémoires*, V, 401.
[36] *Ibid.*, II, 76–77.   [37] *Ibid.*, VI, 10.

tem."[38] Although Bury praised this "divorce from philosophical theory," his interpretation is hardly accurate. For Guizot's history was, to a significant degree, an extension of the Doctrinaire *juste milieu*. And that milieu, if not a system, involved as we have seen both philosophic premises and strategic necessities. When considered in the general context of Doctrinaire thought, Guizot's history reveals in turn some of the same weaknesses which we have seen in other *juste milieu* categories. More than that, it does not seem to promise as sure a route to freedom as one might suppose at first glance.

Guizot himself spoke of his history chair at the Sorbonne as an opportunity "to produce Doctrinaires under the very fire of the enemy."[39] What this meant is clear in the first lesson of his great survey of the origins of representative government. Contemporary views of history were shot through with "errors and abuses." On the one hand, the party of the Revolution expressed either "blind hatred" or "irreverent disdain" for everything ancient. This impiety proved "the herald of superstition." For on the opposite side, the party of the Ancien Regime made the past "an object of idolatrous veneration." "The former desire that society, mutilating its own being, should disown its former life; the latter would have it return to its cradle, in order to remain there immovable and powerless. . . . These . . . find their Utopia in their dreams of the past." True history would avoid both these egregious follies. True history would approach the past with respect, but not servility; with objectivity, but not indifference. For after all, the "study of the past . . . contains nothing which ought to alarm the friends of all that is good and true."[40] Although this is all eminently reasonable,

---

[38] J. B. Bury, *The Idea of Progress* (New York: Macmillan, 1932), pp. 274–75 (italics mine).

[39] Quoted in Pouthas, *op. cit.,* p. 304.

[40] *History of Representative Government,* pp. 7–9.

Guizot has quite clearly done with history what the Doctrinaires did with the political ideas of the *juste milieu*. He has defined true history in terms which make it a defense for the *juste milieu* against the extremes of the Ancien Regime and the Revolution.

In his early historical writings Guizot developed two ideas which ingeniously underpinned this approach: the notions that institutions can only "register" underlying social reality, and that history involves a pattern of determinism.[41] The historian who wishes to know and understand political institutions is "wiser to study society itself first." Only this approach reaches "cause" rather than mere "effect."[42] For legal structure follows, rather than precedes, social structure.[43] To the Ultras who wished to legislate the Revolution out of French history, the warning was explicit. "The causes of revolution are always more general than one supposes."[44] Even those events which seem the work of accident or of a few misguided individuals have hidden sources "far more profound." Behind all history is "a necessary enchainment of events which are constantly born, one after the other, so that the first day carries in its womb the entire future."[45] Although in later years Guizot claimed "for man himself a place, a great place, among the authors of events in the creation of history,"[46] he never completely escaped this idea of determinism. To the end of his life he insisted that history involved certain "laws of higher origin . . . fated causes . . . defined laws of events" which limited "man's free agency."[47]

[41] See Pouthas, *op. cit.*, pp. 310 ff., for a perceptive discussion of these points; also Woodward, *Three Studies of European Conservatism*, pp. 133 ff.

[42] Guizot, *Essais sur l'Histoire de France* (Paris, 1823), p. 87.

[43] *Ibid.*, p. 211. [44] *Ibid.*, p. 67. [45] *Ibid.*

[46] *History of Civilization in France* (New York: Appleton, 1846), II, 86–87; see also *History of Civilization in Europe*, p. 76.

[47] *History of France*, trans. Robert Black (Boston: Aldine, 1886), I, 3 (written 1869).

Whether Guizot got this determinism from Calvin, Savigny, or Hegel,[48] its political utility to the *juste milieu* was obvious. It was not that certain institutions were "necessary" because they could create a desired social order. Rather, they were "necessary" in the sense that the "enchainment" of events made no others possible. The very fact that "progress" was a "law of nature" subjected its realization in political institutions to the limiting terms of nature. In Royer-Collard's words to the Chamber:

There is nothing in what we seem to be debating which has not already long been resolved, accomplished and erected into irrevocable fact, and consequently placed outside the judgment of deliberation. . . . Necessity has its dominion in the moral world, no less than in the physical world. At a given epoch, in a certain state of society, only one type of government is possible for a people.[49]

Translated into the language of politics, Guizot's historical determinism was thus (at least in part) a positional weapon against the right's attempt to resurrect the Ancien Regime and the left's impatience to hurry the present into the future.

If the weapon failed in the real world of politics, Guizot's determinism suggests that even in the world of political theory his concept of history was a doubtful substitute for freedom. The optimism for which he is always celebrated turns out to be more than a little tempered. For if the extremes of right and left could not break the enchainment of history, neither could the men of the *juste milieu*. After all, it was history which had erected the massive contours of the Ancien Regime and the Revolution. The inexorable march of

---

[48] Michel, *op. cit.*, pp. 298–99, credits Savigny and Hegel. Pouthas, *op. cit.*, p. 306, and Johnson, *op. cit.*, p. 333, both note the influence of the former. Although Guizot rejected the particular doctrine of predestination, his Calvinist rearing would seem an equally plausible source.

[49] Barante, *op. cit.*, II, 15–16.

progress might also ultimately level them. But in the meantime reasonable men could apparently do little but cling to that "line at equal distance . . . from right and left." We have already seen what a difficult estate that proved for the Doctrinaires.

In failing as a response to the problem of freedom, Guizot's history does, however, unwittingly provide an explanation for the Doctrinaires' impotence in the realm of politics. For nothing is clearer than that the Doctrinaires themselves did not measure up to the standards which Guizot's history set for the understanding of political events. If those events do indeed only "register" underlying social reality and if "revolutions" invariably involve causes more profound than accident or the mischief of the few, it was obviously the Doctrinaires—not the Ultras or Republicans—who made the most egregious miscalculations in applying the lessons of history to the problems of the present. The theory of the middle class and the July Regime's *pays légal* are the dramatic case in point. It was the Doctrinaires, not their adversaries, who insisted on constructing ideas and institutions that did *not* register reality. Ironically, Guizot the historian proved a most perceptive critic of Guizot the politician!

There is another interesting discrepancy between the middle-class mystique and Guizot's concept of history. In fact, it is analogous to a flaw which one can find also in Marxism. Assuming that conflict has been the driving force behind progress in history, and that progress is to course on into the future, how or why does conflict finally end when one particular class comes to the fore?

The first assumption is one that Guizot elaborated throughout all his history. He invariably attributed Europe's fifteen-century march of progress and conquest of freedom to the "continual struggle" of a "prodigious diversity" of elements within European civilization. Other societies had achieved only passing brilliance because based on a single principle, such as theocracy or democracy, whose potential was quickly exhausted. In Europe the conflict of "classes" was only a recent expression of a more ancient pattern. Guizot traced this pluralism back to the complex of municipal and imperial legacies from Rome, barbarian invasions, feudalism, Church, and monarchy. Through the sweep of history, "all cross, jostle, struggle, interweave" to produce the genius of Europe: progress.[50]

An impressive feature of this analysis is Guizot's general willingness to give each age and element in European history its just due. True, some of his judgments show *juste milieu* bias. For example, he dismissed fifteenth-century France's experiment with the Estates General with a disdain which is perhaps explained only by the Ultras' idealization of the Estates as an alternative to government under the Charter.[51] But such instances are the exception. He credited feudalism with "a vast and salutary influence upon the progress of individual man" and with "the glory of . . . having constantly defended" one most important political idea: "the right of resistance."[52] Despite its abuses the Church had "given to the development of the human mind, in our modern world, an extent and variety which it never possessed elsewhere."[53] In short, "there is no age which does not possess some legitimate claim upon the respect of its descendants."[54] Just as no absolute political power has ever stopped short of tyranny, no one sovereign factor in history has sustained the march of progress and freedom. Like man himself, every era has been a confused crisscross of good and evil which we can never fully understand. If inexorable, progress has been a long, arduous course of struggle.

[50] *History of Civilization in Europe*, pp. 36 ff. and *passim*. See also his comments on his history in *Mémoires*, I, 314; and *Discours Académiques*, pp. 118 ff.
[51] *History of Civilization in Europe*, pp. 251–52.
[52] *Ibid.*, pp. 108–10.   [53] *Ibid.*, p. 152.
[54] *History of Representative Government*, p. 5.

Yet Guizot's theory of the middle class appeared to assume that somehow the struggle would cease once the chosen class fulfilled its destiny. We have already seen that he spoke on occasion as if the "conflict of classes" had already ended.[55] As with the Marxist dialectic, the driving force of history is simply to disappear. All that has explained history in the past becomes superfluous. Progress will continue indefinitely into the future, but its march will now be painless. As for freedom, once the middle class has universalized itself, all men will of course have political rights in addition to civil and economic liberty. One wonders, however, exactly what content liberty will have in the new, all middle-class society. Royer-Collard's belief in "necessary resistances" to power and Guizot's view of history both implied that there is some crucial relation between liberty and diversity. But progress, as projected by Guizot, seemed to be leading men to a world of less rather than more diversity—to a world where a Joseph de Maistre or a Louis Blanc would be a lonely soul indeed. If in such a world Guizot would understandably feel secure in broadening the range of men's liberty, that fact itself suggests an eternal paradox of freedom in general: Regimes and societies usually enlarge freedom only when they are reasonably confident that individuals will exercise it in conformity with certain basic norms, in other words, when those receiving freedom are already unfree in the sense of having been conditioned by common habit, custom, and ideology.

In a sense it may be unfair to labor these problems of the internal consistency of *juste milieu* theory. The Doctrinaires never pretended to have devised a "system" in the sense that Marxism does. Nevertheless, the discrepancy between the middle-class mystique and Guizot's history does represent a fundamental ambiguity in Doctrinaire thought. Was the *juste milieu* to be a progressive mean reached through continuing diversity? Or, like George Eliot's citizen, did the

[55] *Histoire Parlementaire,* III, 556.

Doctrinaires hope for a milieu where "all things . . . find a general level, nowhere in excess"?[56] As we have seen, their concepts of freedom and history suggested the first; their theory of the middle class the second. The ambiguity was never resolved. Perhaps, indeed, it was irresolvable. For it is implicit in the very notion of a "mean" or "middle" position. Such a position must always concede a certain legitimacy to the extremes of which it is a derivative. Guizot himself not only attributed progress to the conflict of extremes; his own political thought was itself a synthesis of categories from left and right. Yet one usually chooses the middle because neither extreme is tolerable. Once entrenched there, one is easily tempted to hope that his own moderation will somehow become universal. When the center is being crushed from both sides, that hope is more than tempting. It becomes compelling. Thus, the Doctrinaires' flight to the middle-class mystique is understandable. It was an irresistible alternative once the "diversity" which they idealized in history had proved a nightmare of virtual civil war in the real world of politics. It was, nevertheless, an alternative which doubly betrayed Guizot's theory of history: first, by violating the imperative that political ideas must reflect reality; second, by abandoning diversity as the route to freedom and progress.

Utility and the Gospel of Manchester

Like the Doctrinaires, the Whigs largely avoided the notion of "natural right" in discussing freedom. The *Edinburgh Review* denied that there was any "sanctuary, or ark, where a catalogue of rights, abstracted from all human circumstances and considerations, has been deposited by nature."[57] For Macaulay freedom, far from being a natural right, was

[56] *Felix Holt* (New York: Century, 1910), epigram for chap. 5, p. 85.
[57] LIII (June 1831), 505.

simply the "lawful birthright of Englishmen." Even the very important right of property was a "creature of the law," and of man-made law.[58] In Brougham one finds the same approach, with a theme of "resistance" reminiscent of Royer-Collard. Liberties of press, public meeting, and jury trial were not only instruments of public enlightenment, but also "reserve powers of the people" which provided an "efficacious check to misgovernment."[59] Only in attacking slavery did Brougham repair to "a law above and prior to all . . . human lawgivers" by which "man can have no property in his fellow creatures." But in practically the next breath he offered as more convincing than "any argument which philosophers can admit" two highly utilitarian "tests or criteria of happiness among any people . . . the progress of population, and the amount of crime."[60]

This utilitarian dimension was important. It saved Whig freedom from the positional negativism and compromise to which I have suggested Doctrinaire freedom often succumbed. Even though not grounded in "natural right," Whig freedom involved a preoccupation with the individual and his self-fulfillment that was largely lacking in Doctrinaire theory. Essentially the Whigs agreed with James Mill's definition of rights as "powers to an individual, which the governing members of the community guarantee" for the "gratification of his desires."[61] If the Whigs were skeptical of the utilitarian *summum bonum*—"the greatest happiness of the greatest number"[62]—which was to determine the allocation of rights, their own solution was scarcely more explicit.

[58] "Mirabeau," *Essays*, III, 68; *Miscellanies*, I, 236 (in House of Commons, Feb. 5, 1841).
[59] *Political Philosophy*, III, 174–89; *Contributions*, II, 424–25.
[60] *Speeches*, I, 427–28 (in House of Commons, July 13, 1830).
[61] James Mill, *Jurisprudence*, reprinted from *Supplement to Encyclopaedia Britannica* (London, 1825), pp. 5, 10.
[62] See, for example, Macaulay, "The Westminster Review's Defence of Mill," *Essays*, II, 89.

As the *Edinburgh Review* theorized, anything deserving the "description of rights" must "contribute to the general happiness of mankind." And the guarantee of particular rights must be based "on the principle of encouraging the formation, development, and protection, of the different sources of enjoyment of which our nature is capable, in direct proportion to the best estimates which we can make of the comparative excellence of these enjoyments."[63] However vague, this did recognize qualitative degrees of "pleasure" and was a more positive approach to freedom than French *juste milieu* theory implied.

Even more important, the very fact that issues could be successfully reduced to terms of "utility" across the broad center sector of English politics meant that the *juste milieu* concept of freedom had some promise of realization in the world of fact. For utility can be a viable standard only if there is some prior agreement on how utility is to be defined. Louis Blanc and Joseph de Maistre would hardly start with similar definitions, but Francis Place and Robert Peel did. Once again the importance of the pervasive consensus on middle-class values which we have seen in English society at large is clear. That consensus had been behind much of the Whig-Tory-Radical collaboration of the Canningite years, as well as the moderate Radicals' support of the Great Reform and their flight from Chartism. Acceptance of middle-class values also explains many of the reforms which the Whigs carried in the first years of their power after 1832. These included abolition of slavery in British colonies, termination of the trading monopoly of the British East India Company, the first annual grant in support of education, extension of political reform to the municipal level, improvement in the administration of justice, and the New Poor Law of 1834, which substituted a workhouse system for the extravagantly expensive practice of granting outdoor relief to able-bodied

[63] LIII (June 1831), 506, 529.

laborers.[64] All this constituted a fairly substantial translation of *juste milieu* freedom from theory to reality.

As the New Poor Law suggests, Whig freedom in the economic realm did not imply a positive state, but rather an essentially laissez faire order. The Whigs fully agreed with the *Westminster Review*'s attitude toward the economic distresses behind Chartism. "The business of government," said Macaulay, "is not directly to make people rich. . . . We can give them only freedom to employ their industry to the best advantage and security in the enjoyment of what their industry has acquired."[65] It was a favorite *Edinburgh Review* argument that the modern workman, having been freed from serfdom, had "forfeited" the protection which the state might justly have afforded him in his earlier condition. Paternalistic interference by legislation meant "a partial return to slavery." It was simply "an attempt to convert the employer of free labour into a slave-owner deprived of his whip."[66] There might be no alternative to relief for "the destitute . . . those unable to work"; but help for those who were merely "poor" placed "a bounty on indolence and vice" and aggravated existing distresses. "As labour is the source of wealth, so is poverty of labour. Banish poverty and you banish wealth."[67]

If all this sounds fully as heartless as Guizot's response to the social problem, there was a crucial difference. The pervasive acceptance of commercial-industrial values gave laissez faire in England something it never had in *juste milieu* France: a certain messianic *élan* which, to a degree, made the cruel side of the new industrial order tolerable. It is undoubtedly true that such "Tory Radical" measures as the law of

---

[64] For general survey of these post-1832 reforms, see Halévy, *History of the English People*, III, 60–129; also Southgate, *op. cit.*, pp. 63–72.

[65] *Miscellanies,* I, 39 (in House of Commons, Sept. 20, 1831).

[66] LXXXIII (Jan. 1846), 87–89.

[67] *Ibid.,* LXIII (July 1836), 487–501.

1833 regulating child labor and the ten-hour law of 1847 also softened the effect of the machine-factory system.[68] But it is difficult to believe that such social legislation was nearly as significant as the widespread conviction that the hardships of the new order were a scant price to pay for the almost unlimited scientific advance, wealth, and comfort which laissez faire would surely bring England. The contrast with France is clear if one turns to those two "freedoms," education and Corn Law repeal, which the *Westminster Review* urged the Chartists to support in place of universal suffrage.

Both the Whigs and the moderate Radicals shared the Doctrinaires' fascination with education and commitment to its public support. Praising extravagantly Guizot's primary education bill of 1833, the *Edinburgh Review* declared, "we should immediately follow the good example of France." What impressed the *Review* about the bill was precisely what the Doctrinaires liked: its promise of securing "uniformity in the groundwork of the intellectual and moral habits of the people . . . that unity of feeling, and nationality, which contributes so much to individual happiness and general prosperity."[69] But here the analogy ends. For in France, as we have seen, *juste milieu* education could be no more than a futile effort to convert a badly fragmentized society to an abstract, difficult synthesis of ideas from the Revolution and the Ancien Regime. In England, however, education for the masses meant neither more nor less than the propagation of the Gospel of Manchester.[70] The exception to the rule of

---

[68] The Whigs were by no means intransigent over such limited regulation. For example, if Brougham opposed the ten-hour law, Macaulay supported it as a legitimate modification of laissez faire. See his *Miscellanies*, II, 98 ff. (in House of Commons, May 22, 1846).

[69] LVIII (Oct. 1833), 19–20, 26.

[70] For Whig hopes that mass education could inculcate "sound ideas of political economy" see Brougham, *Political Philosophy*, I, 18–19; and *Edinburgh Review*, LXXXIII (Jan. 1846), 64.

laissez faire was explicitly designed to prove the truth of the rule. The rule itself was simple, easily understood, and had already proved a catalyst, not a disintegrant, across the wide middle sector of English politics and society. The single movement which, more than any other, succeeded in giving the raw facts of laissez faire the millennial aura of a reform creed was the Anti-Corn Law League. One should follow that statement by immediately noting that the League was by no means a "Whig" crusade, and I will come in a moment to the Whigs' timidity on the issue of repeal. Yet despite that timidity and Cobden's own distrust of the Whigs,[71] the fact remains that the victory for free trade was in the deepest sense a fulfillment of the reform terms of 1832. Macaulay himself expressed that fact not only in supporting repeal, but in later describing 1832 and 1846 as "inseparably associated."[72] For in the Corn Law crusade the middle class, independent of Whig aristocratic leadership, finally exercised the full reality of the power which the Whigs had given it and achieved a degree of class consciousness surpassing even that of 1832. Cobden actually gloried in the class label. If his enemies called him "the Feargus O'Connor of the middle classes," he himself frankly called the League "a middle class set of agitators."[73] As such it was preeminently the most aggressive, brilliantly organized pressure group of nineteenth-century England.

The class consciousness which gave the League militancy, however, did not prevent Cobden and Bright from translating the often crass interests of class into universal, inspirational imperatives. From one end of England to the other, the two men combined laissez faire economics with ap-

[71] See Morley, *op. cit.,* I, 171, 289, 362–63.

[72] *Miscellanies,* II, 171 (at Edinburgh, Nov. 2, 1852). For his support of free trade, see *ibid.,* I, 180 (at Edinburgh, May 29, 1839); and II, 84 (at Edinburgh, Dec. 2, 1845).

[73] Quoted by Asa Briggs, "Middle Class Consciousness in English Politics, 1780–1846," *Past and Present,* I (April 1956), 71.

propriate biblical texts to denounce "pseudo-feudalism," exalt the "nobility of labour," and prove that "trade should be as free as the winds of heaven." Free trade would not only assure all mankind the "fullest abundance of the earth's goods," but in so doing would also carry out "to the fullest extent the Christian doctrine of 'Doing to all men as ye would they should do unto you.'"[74] Even more than that was involved. Free trade and the peace movement, said Cobden, were also "one and the same cause." "The indirect process of Free Trade" was the only hope for eventually ending European colonialism, "the chief source of wars for the last 150 years."[75] To those who asked for still heavier naval armaments to protect British trade, Cobden answered, "Cheapness, not the cannon or the sword, is the weapon through which alone we possess and can hope to defend or extend our commerce." "The more any nation trafficks abroad upon free and honest principles, the less it will be in danger of war."[76]

With that message and the organizational genius of the League, Cobden added the two final strains to the middle-class mystique, elaborating even further the correlation with the Marxist view of the proletariat. Not only was the middle class a general class, produced by historical process and bearing in itself all the true destiny of society at large. Not only would the middle class universalize itself and in so doing dissolve all class lines. In the Corn Law campaign, the middle class also seemed to acquire that solidarity which Marx saw in the proletariat and to promise, ultimately, a world without war. Having cast laissez faire in these messianic terms, Cobden's middle-class agitators, not the menacing masses of Chartism, won the day in *juste milieu* England.

---

[74] Richard Cobden, *Speeches on Questions of Public Policy* (London: T. Fisher Unwin, 1908), I, 198. For inspirational strain of League, see also Asa Briggs, "Cobden and Bright," *History Today*, VII (Aug. 1957), 496–501.

[75] Quoted by Morley, *op. cit.*, I, 230–31.

[76] Richard Cobden, *Political Writings* (London, 1867), I, 292, 299.

The *Westminster Review* had been right. Economic freedom could be a feasible substitute for political democracy.

If in France one can hardly blame the Doctrinaires alone for failing to devise a similarly successful solution, in England one can credit the Whigs only marginally with the triumph of free trade. However alert Macaulay was to the needs of the day and his party, the Whigs in general were timid and reluctant in their acceptance of outright repeal. When Lord Russell announced his "conversion" in 1845, he did indeed suddenly become the "most popular and prominent man of the day," but he scarcely erased the doubts of his party at large.[77] This presents something of a puzzle. If the League and repeal were a fulfillment of the middle-class values which 1832 embodied, how does one explain the Whigs' loss of nerve in the 1840s—a loss of nerve which surely presaged their later demise as a party? It is not enough to say simply that they never adequately transcended their aristocratic origins in an oligarchy of England's great landed families. Macaulay, who came to Whiggery from outside that "privileged enclosure," was only accurate in criticizing Russell's cabinet of December 1845 for being overly exclusive and aristocratic.[78] But the question "why?" remains. Nor is it enough to say that the Whigs' timidity on the Corn Law issue reflected their more general failure in later years to exploit as militantly as they might have the success of the Great Reform. If a strain of uncertainty also runs through their response to demands for further administrative, fiscal, and judicial reform, one still wonders "why."

One possible, if speculative, answer takes us back to the peculiar proclivity of the middling mind to be preoccupied with moderation even when moderation is no longer really a relevant cause. In this sense the very success of the Great Reform proved a subtle trap over the long run for the Whigs. The moderate Radicals' rejection of Chartism and Peel's

---

[77] Southgate, *op. cit.,* p. 128.   [78] *Ibid.,* p. 194.

Tamworth Manifesto might be convincing evidence that the terms of 1832 were safe. But they also meant that the effective left and right both stood within the same broad consensus implicit in those terms. The risk, then, was that either the left or the right, or both, might offer the more militant, meaningful fulfillment of middle-class values and reduce the Whig center to irrelevance. The Whig strategy should have been to retain the initiative it held in the first years after 1832 by aggressively pursuing the free trade cause, when that cause became a popular one with the middle class. Yet the Whigs, true to the character of the middling mind, failed to meet the test. Insisting on moderation in all things, they continued to trim when they should have plunged.[79]

That the Whigs as a party ultimately failed, however, does not blur the very real contrast between the impotence of the French and the viability of the English *juste milieu*. If one can find harbingers in the late 1830s and 1840s of the Whigs' later inability to survive the problems of mass democracy and maturing industrialism, the end did take a long time in coming and the split which Peel caused within Tory ranks in 1846 even seemed for a time to give the Whigs a new lease on life. The Whig *juste milieu* was not crushed from both sides as was the French. What happened, instead, was that Cobden and Peel simply took the middle-class game of 1832 away from the Whigs. The Whigs could never quite understand how this happened, or how Cobden could prefer Peel to themselves. But assuming that the Whigs *had* irretrievably lost their nerve, Cobden and Peel were, in a sense, performing something of a service to the Whig *juste milieu*. For they did cast *juste milieu* freedom in terms which made it a continuing substitute for political democracy.

[79] Although Southgate, *op. cit.,* offers a narrative account of the "passing" of the Whigs rather than an analysis of the problem of middlingness, he reaches much the same conclusion in suggesting that the Whigs were simply *too* moderate (see p. 161).

Macaulay on History

History was one Whig asset which Macaulay refused to let Cobden and Peel preempt. It also provides the final correlation between Whig and Doctrinaire thought. Like Guizot, Macaulay believed that history involved some immanent law of progress. But Macaulay's belief was no uncertain substitute for freedom. It was rather a virtual enshrinement of the values of 1832 and 1846. The Whigs as a party may have lost their nerve in implementing middle-class liberties, but not Macaulay when he turned to interpreting history. His proclivity for politicizing the past even offended Guizot:

On reading him, I often feel the regret of meeting in history the spirit of party politics. . . . When we look back into the past, when we re-open tombs, we owe to the dead we draw from them, complete and scrupulous justice. In bringing them again upon the stage, we ought to revive the ideas and sentiments they exhibited there. In assigning their respective parts, we should equitably distinguish their personal interests and rights, and not mix up with their ashes the living coals of our own hearth. Lord Macaulay has not always obeyed this law of historical equity and truth.[80]

The gist of Guizot's objection has often been stated even more strongly by latter-day critics who portray Macaulay as the example par excellence of what Herbert Butterfield dubs the "Whig interpretation of history." To follow Butterfield, Whig history is "the study of the past with direct and perpetual reference to the present." Its method is to abridge the "complexity of human change" and the "richness of . . . the concrete life of the past" by finding in history "an obvious principle of progress, of which the Protestants and Whigs have been the perennial allies while the Catholics and

[80] *Embassy to St. James*, p. 249.

Tories have perennially formed obstruction." Far from trac-
ing the secret of progress to the "interplay and perpetual
collision" of these forces, the Whig historian dismisses the
obstruction as having contributed "nothing to the making of
the present-day." Finally, by organizing all history with reference to the present, the Whig endows the values of the
present with a "finality and absoluteness" which permit him
confidently to pass moral judgment on the past.[81]

Whatever the shortcomings of his history, all this would be
less than a fair appraisal of Guizot. For him the very conflicts
which Butterfield's Whig would regard as imperiling progress were its driving force. It is this non-Whiggism in Guizot's history which raises the problem of how progress is to
continue once one class has inherited the earth and ended
conflict.

The more obvious question is how close Macaulay himself
is to Butterfield's model. Although he is a good deal closer
than Guizot, some interesting qualifications emerge if one
looks objectively at the full range of Macaulay's historical
works. For example, when theorizing *about* history, Macaulay almost seemed to anticipate Butterfield by scorning any
single factor analysis of the past. In his 1828 essay on "History," he offered an explanation for the rise of European
civilization rather similar to Guizot's. With the breakup of
the Roman Empire, Europe had become a "great federal
community" whose states were "united by the easy ties of
international law and a common religion." Far more

[81] *The Whig Interpretation of History* (London: G. Bell and Sons,
1951), pp. vi, 12–13, 21, 35, 41, 68, 107. Although Butterfield is curiously
shy about naming the Whigs whom he is attacking, Macaulay is clearly a
major target. For other treatments of the same theme, see H. A. L. Fisher,
op. cit.; R. L. Schuyler, "Macaulay and His History," *Political Science
Quarterly,* LXIII (June 1948), 161 ff.; and Pieter Geyl, "Macaulay," in his
Debates With Historians (London: Batsford, 1955), pp. 19 ff. For dis-
senting comment from the Butterfield view, note H. R. Trevor-Roper,
Men and Events (New York: Harpers, 1957), pp. 249 ff.

significant than these common bonds, however, were the "widely different" national institutions, languages, literatures, manners, and systems of education. Like Guizot, Macaulay found that the interplay of these diverse influences had saved Europe from "a uniformity fatal to all development. . . . Competition has produced activity where monopoly would have produced sluggishness."[82]

To understand this development Macaulay insisted that history must not mistake so-called important events as the only stuff of human existence. Again like Guizot, he believed that the great revolutions which so often fascinate historians are only the "consequences of hidden changes already consummated in the mysterious complex of society itself." To explore these hidden revolutions the historian may often have to reclaim "those materials which the novelist has appropriated." Just as important as armies and senates are "the fine shades of national character . . . ordinary men as they appear in their ordinary business and in their ordinary pleasures . . . the convivial table and the domestic hearth. . . vulgar expressions . . . even the retreats of misery." Most important, once below the surface of events, the historian must avoid the error of distorting facts "to suit general principles." "In every human character and transaction there is a mixture of good and evil."[83]

However sound and like Butterfield's these thoughts were, Macaulay was not always true to them. In the polemics of some of his other historical essays we enter a world of such black and white simplicity that his detractors begin to seem justified in their harshness. For when he turned from the theory to the writing of history, Macaulay did delight in looking back over England's past and finding one vast movement of progress leading inexorably to the great crest of 1832. Often the implication was that all resistance to that tide had been sheer obstruction. Progress had occurred *despite,* not

[82] *Essays,* I, 417–18.   [83] *Ibid.,* pp. 419–32.

because of struggle. As he declared in his essay on Mackintosh, the question for the historian to ask about men of the past was, quite simply, "Were their faces set in the right or the wrong direction?"

Each of those great and ever memorable struggles, Saxon against Norman, Villein against Lord, Protestant against Papist, Roundhead against Cavalier, Dissenter against Churchman, Manchester against Old Sarum, was . . . a struggle on the result of which were staked the dearest interests of the human race; and every man who . . . distinguished himself on the *right side,* is entitled to our gratitude and respect.[84]

Those who had been on the "wrong side" did not always receive that mercy which Macaulay seemed to promise in saying that every man was a mixture of both good and evil. All too often men became either good or evil. As he scathingly disposed of Charles I: "A good father! A good husband! Ample apologies indeed for 15 years of persecution, tyranny, and falsehood! . . . For ourselves, we own that *we do not understand the common phrase, a good man, but a bad king.*"[85]

But Macaulay's essays alone fall far short of being a fair measure of his history. Too many were written in the rashness of youth or partisan debate. If his political creed of Whiggism remained unchanged, his later *History of England* was a far more mature, balanced achievement, which in some respects fulfilled Macaulay's original theory of how history ought to be written. In contrast with the essays we find here, for example, repeated praise for the Church's great service in preserving through the Dark Ages the precious "germ from which a second and more glorious civiliza-

[84] "Sir James Mackintosh's History of the Revolution," *Essays,* III, 276, 279–81 (italics mine).
[85] "Milton," *Essays,* I, 240–41 (italics mine).

tion was to spring."[86] Here also is a sense for the irony of history. The fifteenth-century military reverses which forced England to give up hope of a continental empire are described as "blessings in the guise of disasters" which enabled future generations to turn their energy to nobler objects.[87] Again, if Charles I is still a tyrant, Macaulay now declares that it is his very tyranny to which "our country owes its freedom." Charles himself is even credited with "some of the qualities of a good, and even a great prince," including the ability to face death with "regal dignity" and "dauntless courage."[88]

As all this suggests, the Macaulay of the *History* no longer divided English political development into obvious "right" and "wrong" sides. As for Whigs and Tories, he observed at the outset:

The truth is that, though both parties have often seriously erred, England could have spared neither. If, in her institutions, freedom and order, the advantages arising from innovation and the advantages arising from prescription, have been combined to an extent elsewhere unknown, we may attribute this happy peculiarity to the strenuous conflicts and alternate victories of two rival confederacies of statesmen, a confederacy zealous for authority and antiquity, and a confederacy zealous for liberty and progress.[89]

This was not mere lip service which Macaulay conveniently forgot as soon as he plunged into the saga of the English Revolution. On the contrary, he was quite candid in admitting that such constitutional issues as Charles II's use of the dispensing power and the distinction between "rightful" and "wrongful" resistance were hardly matters of black and white.[90] Nor was the happy resolution of those issues an ex-

[86] *History of England*, I, 8, 22–24, 44–48.   [87] *Ibid.*, p. 20.
[88] *Ibid.*, pp. 82, 93, 126.   [89] *Ibid.*, p. 99.
[90] *Ibid.*, p. 223; IV, 6, 228.

clusively Whig achievement. He castigated the Whigs for the "unscrupulous and hot-headed" revolt of 1683 against Charles II and the "illegal and impudent schemes" to overthrow James II two years later.[91] Moreover, the praise which the Whigs did receive was shared with a host of Tory Cavaliers like the Earl of Danby, the Duke of Ormond, Sir Edward Seymour, and Heneage Finch. Who was Macaulay's own particular hero from the Revolution? Interestingly enough, George Savile, Marquess of Halifax, the "trimmer" par excellence, committed to neither great party, but the servant on different occasions of both.[92]

Whatever one may think of Macaulay's judgment, this is surely not to do all that Butterfield charged. It is surely not to explain either 1688 or English history in general with any one simple principle of which "Protestants and Whigs have been the perennial allies while Tories and Catholics have perennially formed obstruction."

However, as the case of Halifax may suggest, even the late Macaulay did judge the past with rather persistent reference to the present. If he conceded that progress in the past had come out of diversity and struggle, he resorted invariably to the values of the present in determining what was or was not progress. The important fact was not whether Halifax was a Whig or Tory, but rather that he had occupied an intermediate position comparable to the Whigs of the Reform era and that "he almost invariably took the view of the great questions of his time which history has finally adopted."[93] In turn, the genius of 1688 was not so much its Whig pedigree as the fact that it contained the seed of "every good law" passed in the succeeding 150 years — above all, the seed of 1832.[94]

This approach to the past through the terms of the present

[91] *Ibid.,* I, 263; II, 241 ff.; III, 30.
[92] *Ibid.,* III, 80 ff., 285, 312, 323, 383; V, 17.
[93] *Ibid.,* IX, 8.   [94] *Ibid.,* IV, 265.

is blatantly clear even in Macaulay's celebrated chapter on "the state of England in 1685." True, the chapter did fulfill his early promise to explore the "mysterious complex of society itself." But what is even more striking than the detail of his description is his relentless comparison of every facet of "old England" with his own day to the disparagement of the past. Formerly, even among lords of the manor, "language and pronunciation were such as we should expect to hear only from the most ignorant clowns." Knights of the shire had libraries no better than "may now perpetually be found in the servants' hall." Those who know the "blazing splendor" of Victorian London "may perhaps smile" at the lighting of 1685. Macaulay himself smiles condescendingly at Pepys for noting as "a wonder" that from the center of Bristol one's view of the fields was entirely shut out by houses. "His standard was not high." Bristol then occupied "but a small portion of the land on which it now stands." Again, even the sheep and oxen were "diminutive" in comparison with those "now driven to our markets."[95] All this continues almost ad infinitum. Seldom does Macaulay express any Rankian feeling of awe for the past in the sense of suggesting that every age is "immediate to God . . . in its own self." Throughout, the major theme is to judge and belittle by comparison with the present.

Thus, even if the Butterfield thesis is perhaps unjustly harsh, it is not unfair to say that Macaulay's history did seem to claim for the values of middle-class Victorian materialism something of that same "finality" which he attributed politically to the Great Reform. Progress would indeed carry on into the future. "We too shall be outstripped."[96] But this was false humility to the large degree that Macaulay assumed that the course of that progress was already determined by the very nineteenth-century values which enabled him to judge

[95] *Ibid.*, II, 36, 41, 56–57, 62, 82, 112.   [96] *Ibid.*, p. 145.

the past so confidently. That assumption was an even more flagrant betrayal of his professed belief in a diversity and conflict of values than one finds in Guizot. Those who questioned the new era, who talked of "degeneracy and decay," who looked back to a golden age which existed "only in their imagination" were simply foolish.[97] If Guizot might well have sympathized with Southey's idealization of old agricultural England vis à vis the "wen" of industrialism, not Macaulay. Imagine the imbecility of preferring rose bushes and weather-stained cottages to "steam engines and independence." Imagine the imbecility of Southey's test of the old and the new orders: "To stand on a hill, to look at a cottage and a factory, and to see which is the prettier."[98] It is simply "unreasonable and ungrateful in us to be constantly discontented with a condition that is constantly improving."[99] With that, history became virtually a magic potion which could legitimize and finalize the freedom granted by 1832 and 1846.

If in retrospect the extravagant optimism of Macaulay's history surely seems rather more galling than the tempered hopefulness of Guizot's, one final word of excuse should perhaps be offered for the Whig. This is that the temptation to overconfidence was far greater for Macaulay than Guizot. The year 1688 had proved superlatively successful. That was more than any Doctrinaire could claim for 1789. In the end, France's 1848 convinced Guizot that even 1830 had been a disastrous precedent.[100] In contrast, England's relatively tranquil passage through the 1840s not only seemed to justify Macaulay's faith in 1832; it must also have seemed to confirm the rightness of judging the past in terms of the present. Guizot's flight to the middle-class mys-

[97] *Ibid.*, I, 2–3.
[98] "Southey's Colloquies on Society," *Essays*, II, 149, 177.
[99] *History of England*, II, 145.
[100] See, for example, his *Mémoires*, II, 18–19, and compare with earlier view in *Histoire Parlementaire*, I, 156.

tique from the diversity and struggle which he found in history reflected the failure of French *juste milieu* freedom in the real world. Macaulay's enshrinement in history of the values of the chosen class reflected, despite the Whigs' failure of nerve, the very real success of English *juste milieu* freedom.

Chapter Five

CONCLUSION

Human Irony

EVEN in a study largely of ideas, rather than of men, the individual political fates of the four theorists with whom we started are not without interest and lead appropriately to a more general summing-up of the problem of middlingness. In France, Royer-Collard's retirement from active political life after 1830 reflected not only his sixty-seven years of age, but also his exhaustion and disillusion with the struggles of the Restoration. Clearly he had had a moment of truth after the July Days when he remarked, "I am among the conquerors, but the victory is sad indeed."[1] For if Royer-Collard, as president of the Chamber of Deputies, had himself been an activist in the overthrow of Charles X, he realized that the July Days meant more than the failure of his beloved Charter of 1814. They also meant that the new *juste milieu* regime had the unfortunate parentage of revolution and faced a continuing siege from right and left. That was a battle from which Royer-Collard understandably withdrew to the sidelines. Although his brief reappearance to oppose the September Laws of 1835 was dramatic proof that he did not always sanction the "necessities" to which the July Regime was driven, the future leadership of the *juste milieu* had passed to the younger generation of Guizot.

Guizot's fate, both as a statesman and a political theorist, was precisely that of the July Regime itself. He succumbed inexorably to the strategic, intellectual, and psychological attrition of a losing siege and was swept from office by revolution in 1848. As the *Edinburgh Review* said of him in later years, "He seems to have been formed for resistance."

[1] Barante, *op. cit.,* II, 446.

Despite his great services in opposing both Ultra Royalism and Jacobinism, "this habit of mind and policy became in the end his greatest danger, for it was protracted until the monarchy itself perished under the strain."[2] With his political career at an end after 1848, Guizot's thought and writing turned more and more from the worldly to the religious realm. And that, perhaps, is where the middling mind does find its ultimate solace.

If one listened only to Macaulay's critics, one might suspect that he too met an unhappy fate. Walter Bagehot, for example, wrote of him:

His mind shows no trace of change. What he is, he was; and what he was, he is. He early attained a high development, but he has not increased it since: years have come, but they have whispered little; as was said of the second Pitt, "He never grew, he was cast." . . . His first speeches are as good as his last, his last scarcely richer than his first. He came into public life at an exciting season, he shared of course in that excitement, and the same excitement still quivers in his mind. . . . He is still the man of '32: . . . The events of twenty years have been full of rich instruction . . . but they have not instructed him,—his creed is a fixture.[3]

This harsh criticism carried more than a little truth. Macaulay himself assured his electors at Edinburgh in 1839, "My opinions are still what they were when, in 1831 and 1832, I took part . . . in that great pacific victory which purified the representative system of England."[4] Again in 1845, "My opinions, from the day on which I entered public life, have never varied."[5]

But Bagehot's barbs missed an even more important truth: Macaulay's creed, though a fixture, served quite well to keep

[2] CVIII (Oct. 1858), 415.
[3] Walter Bagehot, "Thomas Babington Macaulay," *Works*, II, 62–63.
[4] *Miscellanies*, I, 170 (at Edinburgh, May 29, 1839).
[5] *Ibid.*, II, 84 (at Edinburgh, Dec. 2, 1845).

him at the vital center of English politics. He not only held high office under both Melbourne and Russell, but won landslide election to Parliament at Edinburgh a full twenty years after the Great Reform without even appearing before his electors. Although his Whig view of English history dated back to the 1820s,[6] when his formal *History* was published in 1848, it outsold the latest popular novels. Obviously the creed of 1832—militantly pursued—was still the *right* creed. For as we have seen, the decades after the Great Reform simply did not work the revolutionary changes in English politics that they did in French. However merciless Bagehot might be, politics were relatively kind to Macaulay.

If the fates of Royer-Collard, Guizot, and Macaulay present no serious puzzle, Brougham's story after 1832 does. And the puzzle is worth more than passing mention. For when Brougham's fate is projected against the background of our study of middlingness, a somewhat revisionist view of his fall from grace seems to emerge, and a final note of irony is added to the contrast of the Whig and Doctrinaire *justes milieux*.

Leslie Stephen, in his discussion of Whiggism, disposed of Brougham with only a footnote:

I need not speak of Brougham, then the most conspicuous advocate of Whiggism. He published . . . a *Political Philosophy,* which, according to Lord Campbell, killed the "Society for the Diffusion of Useful Knowledge.". . . The book was bad enough to kill, if a combination of out-worn platitudes can produce that effect.[7]

Since most books by Whigs were apt to be dull, Stephen's treatment of Brougham does not quite satisfy. But one can

___

[6] For example, his "Milton" (written in 1825) in *Essays,* I, 202 ff. See also reference to his 1822 Cambridge prize essay on William III, in G. O. Trevelyan, *Life and Letters of Macaulay* (Oxford University Press, 1932), I, 78–79.   [7] *The English Utilitarians* (London, 1900), II, 108.

guess that the real explanation is that by the late 1830s Brougham had managed to alienate himself from the very *juste milieu* which, in 1832, he had been "conspicuous" in creating. After being, in Macaulay's judgment, "the most popular man in England"[8] in 1830 and serving as Lord Chancellor for four years, Brougham was excluded from the second Melbourne cabinet in 1835 and never again held office. In 1836 he attended the House of Lords not a single time. His contributions to the *Edinburgh Review* thinned to a trickle compared with earlier years. In 1838, thirty years before his death, the still definitive edition of his speeches was published. Although in 1812 he had won one of the first great victories for English industry over land in securing repeal of the Orders in Council, he played only an insignificant, ambiguous part in repeal of the Corn Laws.[9] As Charles Greville wrote of him in later years:

When one thinks of the greatness of his genius and the depth of his fall, from the loftiest summit of influence, power, and fame, to the lowest abyss of political degradation, in spite of the faults and follies of his character and conduct, one cannot help feeling regret and compassion at the sight of such a noble wreck and of so much glory obscured.[10]

Why did he fall? Hardly, as Stephen seemed to imply, from dullness. Rather, "his character and conduct" do seem the obvious reason. Always an opportunist and meddler in matters not his own concern, Brougham at last exceeded all bounds of propriety. In November 1834, when Melbourne's first government was to be succeeded by Peel's, Brougham—without consulting his colleagues—made the extraordinary offer to his successor, Lord Lyndhurst, to take the subordinate office of Chief Baron of the Exchequer in the

[8] G. O. Trevelyan, *Life of Macaulay*, I, 174.
[9] Norman McCord, *The Anti-Corn Law League* (London: Allen & Unwin, 1958), pp. 19–39.
[10] Quoted by A. Aspinall, *Lord Brougham and the Whig Party*, p. 218.

new Tory cabinet. His explanation was that his appointment as Chief Baron would save the Crown the annual pension of 5000 pounds to which he would be entitled as an ex-Lord Chancellor out of office! Whatever his true motives, the offer was a blunder which drew ridicule from the Tories and badly embarrassed the Whigs. Moreover the Whigs had little reason to be charitable, since the Lyndhurst affair came hard on the heels of an only slightly less offensive display of infidelity by Brougham. During the summer of 1834 he had made a sensational, demogogic tour of Scotland on which he steered a rather wide range of the political compass, depending on his audience; he sharply criticized several of his colleagues and boasted, with extreme impropriety, of his familiarity with the King. Although the grand political tour was to become something of an institution in British politics of a later day, in 1834 sound Whigs looked on the novelty with suspicion and on Brougham's personal conduct with horror. When the Whigs returned to power the following year, Melbourne had fair reason to find a new Lord Chancellor. Brougham never succeeded in regaining Whig trust, and this saga of eccentricity, impropriety, and inordinate ambition has usually satisfied his biographers as ample explanation for his fall.[11]

Yet, to draw somewhat speculatively upon the comparative French-English study which we have just made, I would suggest that the conventional explanation misses what may have been another equally significant reason for Brougham's continued alienation from the very Whig *juste milieu* which he had helped create. In French parlance of the day, Brougham was a man of "movement" rather than "resistance."

[11] *Ibid.*, pp. 204 ff. See also Russell's judgment of Brougham's character in the former's *Recollections and Suggestions,* pp. 136–40; John Lord Campbell, *Lives of Lord Lyndhurst and Lord Brougham* (London, 1869), pp. 446 ff.; Frances Hawes, *Henry Brougham* (London: Jonathan Cape, 1957), pp. 259–260. Chester New, *op. cit.,* takes Brougham's career only through 1830.

Although he never abandoned his *juste milieu* concepts of the mixed state, the sovereignty of reason, and utilitarian liberty, he refused in later years to stick to the Whig tenet that 1832 was a "permanent" settlement. Through his years as Earl Grey's Lord Chancellor, the course of Brougham's ideas kept him at the center of Whiggism. His mistake was that after the Reform battle, he continued to move, while, as Macaulay proved, the terms of 1832 stood still. If Whig timidity on the Corn Law issue was a miscalculation, it was a far greater miscalculation to question 1832 itself. Yet that is what Brougham did. By 1839, in what has been a curiously overlooked pamphlet, he was already attacking Russell's declarations against further "organic change" and denying that the franchise "should be limited by property, to the exclusion of the most industrious and skillful members of the community."[12] In the 1840s, in the very book whose platitudes annoyed Stephen, he again castigated the "gross absurdity" of the property qualification and called for "a very large extension of the franchise" through the establishment of educational tests.[13] By 1848 he had even reached the judgment that the middle classes were "not more deserving" and "certainly . . . much less independent, than the good workmen."[14] The *Edinburgh Review* was sufficiently shocked by this kind of talk to call his proposals "practically . . . universal suffrage . . . a revolution."[15]

The irony is that just this kind of "movement" might well have saved the French *juste milieu* in the 1840s. And perhaps it is not entirely idle to wonder whether Brougham and Guizot might not have ended their careers more happily had they somehow managed to trade places. Interestingly

[12] *Reply to Lord John Russell's Letter to the Electors of Stroud* (London, 1839), p. 5 and *passim*.

[13] *Political Philosophy*, III, 71 ff.

[14] Brougham, *Letter to the Marquess of Lansdowne* (London, 1848), p. 165.

[15] LXXXI (Jan. 1845), pp. 38–39.

enough, if Guizot admired the English, Brougham loved France and founded the English colony at Cannes. In 1848, the year Feargus O'Connor returned to England from the Continent, Brougham even applied for dual English-French citizenship so that he could enter French politics![16]

Although it is surely possible to dismiss Brougham's "movement" as simply more "opportunism," the *Edinburgh Review* did not, and to do so would probably be less than fair. For example, even in the 1840s Brougham still balked at popular demand for the secret ballot. Moreover, as we have seen, agitation for broadening the franchise hardly proved a profitable enterprise in post-1832 English politics. Whatever advantage electoral concession might have brought the French *juste milieu,* the really opportunistic course in England was to follow Macaulay: stand by "finality."

That fact suggests that however one judges his sincerity, Brougham seriously misunderstood the political milieu in which he was operating as the years went by after the Great Reform. His friend Croker hinted as much in advising him: "When we come to . . . further democratic reforms . . . you will be in your place and have room and solid ground for all your exertions."[17] If Whiggism in general failed to see the need for militant fulfillment of middle-class values in the Corn Law fight, Brougham failed to grasp the intrinsic viability of the 1832 settlement. He did not realize that the day of democracy had not quite come. When it did, the Whigs as a party might indeed fail. But in the meantime, the only strategy was to play the middle-class game. Although this misunderstanding does not condone Brougham's improprieties in Scotland, it may explain in part why he undertook a grand political tour which would really have been appropriate only in post-1867 England.

Another illustration of this same point is Brougham's fail-

[16] Aspinall, *op. cit.,* p. 222.   [17] *The Croker Papers,* II, 303.

ure in later years to reassess fully the analogy which he had drawn between French and English politics during the Reform Bill struggle. Writing of the French Revolution of 1848, he declared that the experience "makes all established governments insecure—shakes to its foundation all confidence in existing constitutions." What impressed him was that the French upheaval had been "prompted by no felt inconvenience,—announced by no complaint." If revolution could come in such an "extempore" fashion, no government "can now be held safe for an hour," not even that of England if she became "infected with the fever which has mastered reason in other countries." Those who pretended that there was no such danger in England were simply guilty of "folly" and "arrogance."[18]

All this was not only to miss the deep political and social discontent which toppled Guizot's narrowly based regime; by implication, Brougham also seemed to discount heavily the significant stability and consensus which the years after 1832 had revealed within the broad middle sector of English politics. When Brougham wrote in 1848, Feargus O'Connor had already proved that the British Constitution could not be blown away by "a sudden blast of the popular gale." Part of its stability was surely the genius of the British ruling class for compromise. To that Brougham also seemed blind. In later years, referring to the "Aristocratic Mysteries" of party, he condemned both Tories and Whigs as perverse conspiracies which "render the people only tools and instruments of an oligarchy."[19] Perhaps, again, this was mere recrimination for his own treatment by Melbourne. Yet it may also have reflected a basic confusion bordering on hallucination concerning the England of his day. At times one suspects that Brougham saw himself as a latter-day Talleyrand, operating

[18] "Of Revolutions: Particularly that of 1848," *Works of Lord Brougham,* VIII, 270, 280, 332.
[19] "Effects of Party," *Works,* III, 373, 382.

in a fragmentized, disintegrating political system. Fearful of revolution and distrustful of aristocracy, he seemed still to have the early Whig vision of a "chasm" in English politics—a chasm which could be bridged only by further political reform. In this sense, despite Brougham's "movement" after 1832, one can argue that he was still thinking in terms of middlingness.

One might conclude that Brougham was the victim not only of his own character, but also of that subtle occupational hazard of the center: miscalculating the extremes which one is trying to compromise. On second thought, perhaps the word "hazard" should be qualified. For if the early Whig view of the "chasm" had itself been somewhat distorted, it had probably erred on the side of safety by encouraging the men of '32 to grant a more generous, lasting reform than they would otherwise have done. But as the careers of both Brougham and O'Connor suggest, it was quite another matter in the 1840s to mistake England for France. Rather than providing a margin of safety, it was a passport to political suicide. The fact that this was precisely Brougham's fate, however, does not mean that he has been misplaced in our gallery of *juste milieu* theorists. On the contrary, his very fate dramatizes in human irony the contrast between the French and English *justes milieux* and the importance of the middle-class creed which Brougham had held as a "man of '32."

The Paradox of the Center

To close with this underlining of the French-English contrast, however, would hardly do justice to the problem or material which we have studied. If the *Edinburgh Review* was content at mid-century to abandon its early view of a direct analogy between the Doctrinaire and Whig political positions and proudly proclaim superior English genius in politics,[20] we cannot leave matters at that. For that reassessment, valid as far as it went, missed the fact that in a significant sense the original analogy of Whig and Doctrinaire ideas was still the basic point of reference. English optimism at mid-century did seem to reflect only the difference between France and England. But had the two national experiences been totally irrelevant to one another, the contrast could have no meaning. The bare fact that one country suffered revolution in 1848 while the other did not proved nothing by itself. What made that fact meaningful was that France's 1830 and England's 1832 had, after all, attempted to establish remarkably similar theories of middle-class rule as a *juste milieu* between revolution and reaction. It was that analogy of ideas which gave the English some reason for pride in their own relatively happy passage through the 1840s. They had been successful with *juste milieu* ideas; the French had not. In turn, our projection of that analogy of ideas against the contrasting political and social backgrounds on either side of the Channel has, hopefully, brought us to some conclusions about the problem of middlingness in general.

One thing is obvious: the implications of the middling way have turned out to be more subtle and complicated than the usual Aristotelian rubrics would lead us to believe. The paradox suggested at the outset apparently carries more than a little truth. Middlingness does seem to prove least realistic where it is most relevant, and least relevant where it is most realistic.

In the first context, the polity rent between two formidable extremes, we have seen that the unrealism of the center position will involve rather more than the obvious strategic danger of being crushed from both sides. The center will also

[20] See, for example, LXXXIX (April 1849), 558–73; LXXXXII (Oct. 1850), 521.

be under a double disadvantage in terms of ideology and psychology. First, it will find that the extremes possess a crucial initiative in laying down the ideological categories of dispute and that its own ideas will be essentially a positional, defensive response to that initiative. Second, those ideas will, more likely than not, be shot through and through with unreality.

If these two points seem contradictory at first glance, they really are not. Assuming that the center's ideological categories are already determined for it and reflect the existence of formidable extremes, the center will usually attempt to camouflage the true state of affairs. It will do so by recasting its categories in terms which seem to transcend not only the center's untenable position in the world of politics, but also the basic contradictions which any synthesis of ideas from far right and far left is certain to involve. In Doctrinaire thought, the extravagant faith in the power of sweet reasonableness, the mystic eulogy of the Charter, the middle-class mystique, and the tacit mistaking of France for England all illustrate this tactic. Unwitting or not, they can all be considered attempts to make the middling position appear realistic as well as relevant. But at the same time they were themselves a flight from reality which deluded only the Doctrinaires.

As such, Doctrinaire thought surely suggests that the old cliché that political ideas "mirror" their environment in some direct fashion is hardly adequate. Although there are probably more profound and confusing ways of expressing the point, perhaps it suffices here to say that if political ideas sometimes do mirror social and political reality, they can also be a kind of dream fantasy of what is not reality. Despite the center's perennial claim to a practical, common sense approach to political ideas, the realism-relevance problem gives it a built-in proclivity to theorize in unreal terms. If that statement seems a truism in a context like *juste milieu* France, I would offer two excuses for laboring the point.

First, it is a truism which is curiously obscured by all the Aristotelian platitudes concerning the middle way. Second, as I have suggested before and will again in a moment, the middling mind demonstrates this same proclivity in circumstances far more friendly than the Doctrinaires faced.

To turn briefly from middlingness in general to the middle class in particular, Aristotle again fares poorly in *juste milieu* France. Like other middle classes which have stood in isolation and peril, Guizot's beloved bourgeoisie did not embody the Aristotelian virtues of "reason" and "moderation." Those virtues, where they exist, are clearly not derivatives of the class per se, but rather of the total milieu in which the class exists. Although Aristotle felt that there was something virtuous about moderate wealth per se and assumed that the rich and poor would "not serve each other," he did seem to recognize the importance of the broader societal context when he admitted that the middle-class state can be viable only if what is identified as that class is also the dominant element in the polity. If he failed to elaborate the point, the reason is perhaps not far to find. The Greek city state was generally a close-knit society with a value structure which overarched all classes. Given that relatively friendly clime, Aristotle can perhaps be forgiven for not laboring the importance of the total social milieu of his chosen class. The Doctrinaires, however, cannot be forgiven so easily. Since nineteenth-century France obviously lacked an overarching value structure, nothing should have been more apparent to the Doctrinaires than the need for hardheaded examination of society at large and for generous, rather than narrow, enfranchisement of the bourgeoisie.

What Aristotle said about the middle-class state suggests again the converse of the paradox of the center in general. Where is it most realistic to theorize in terms of a vital center? The answer is the polity whose effective left and right do stand within or can be brought within the same value consensus. As we have seen, the pervasive acceptance of commercial-industrial values in English society at large was crucial underpinning for the Whig *juste milieu*. That consensus meant that the Whig concepts of sovereignty, representation, freedom, and history had fairly substantial political and social reality to trade on. It also meant that the middle class itself, in contrast to Guizot's bourgeoisie, was a confident, burgeoning, responsible order.

But even with that measure of success, a center is still very likely to face serious problems over the longer run. Precisely because the effective left and right share the center's fundamental values, they may easily render the center irrelevant by offering a more meaningful realization of those values. The center's very triumph over extremism thus places it in peril, unless it can provide a continuing *raison d'être* for middlingness. Granted that the Whig *juste milieu* was in 1832 both a relevant and realistic center, the conjuring up of more dangerous extremes than in fact existed through the identification with France perhaps reflected, again unwittingly or not, the middling mind's attempt to avoid the fate of irrelevance. But like the Doctrinaire attempt to appear realistic, the Whig tactic was also a flight from reality. And as the years went by, it became a fairly transparent, hazardous solution to the problem of relevance. Brougham's latter-day view of English politics and his premature questioning of the 1832 settlement proved that point. When a center has proved realistic, an attempt to relocate it is no way to preserve its relevance. The far safer course is to try to retain the initiative from left and right by pursuing militantly, rather than hesitantly, the values implicit in the original *juste milieu* synthesis. But as we have seen, even that course is quite likely to offend the middling mind's craving for moderation in all things. The middling mind seems often to prefer the slow death of irrelevance. And one can argue that it was that kind of death which the Whigs themselves began to suffer during the very years when the triumph of their *juste milieu* seemed so permanent.

That the English as well as the French *juste milieu* did ultimately fail perhaps seems to document Karl Mannheim's argument that a middle class is by nature incapable of a viable "synthesis" of the diverse intellectual and political positions which post-feudal Western society has encompassed. Mannheim, however, approaches the problem of *juste milieu* on a rather different track than has my analysis. His basic premise is the crucial importance of class in determining the style and content of thought. As he puts it, all those bound to a particular class "have their outlooks and activities directly and exclusively determined by their specific social situations." Although the concept of "inherent" ideology does not seem inconsistent with that proposition, what Mannheim emphasizes is the inability of a fixed class to propound ideas which can ever transcend its own interests in a dynamic, comprehensive synthesis. In the case of a middle class, "threatened from above and below," the attempted synthesis will be what the *juste milieu* was—a static, dead level mediation of extremes. What group *is* capable of "true synthesis"? Mannheim suggests "only . . . a relatively class-less stratum not too firmly situated in the social order"—what Alfred Weber called the "socially unattached intelligentsia."[21]

One is tempted to make at least several passing comments on the Mannheim thesis. First, the fact that two such remarkably different groups as the French bourgeoisie and the English middle class could produce such remarkably similar *juste milieu* ideologies suggests that the relation between class base and political thought may be rather more complicated than Mannheim indicates. Second, although the description "threatened from above and below" may well be accurate for the French bourgeoisie, it hardly fits the English

[21] *Ideology and Utopia,* pp. 153 ff.

middle class at mid-nineteenth century. Mannheim himself declares that any successful synthesis "must permeate the broadest reaches of social life, must take natural root in society." And indeed that was what the middle-class values of the English *juste milieu* seemed to do. Even in the case of the French bourgeoisie, matters are not too simple. If it was "threatened," it was also so badly fragmentized that one can doubt that it was really a "class" at all or that it occupied the "fixed" position in the simple three-tier social structure which Mannheim seems to imply. Third, however much our four *juste milieu* theorists idealized the middle class, in a curious way they themselves were somewhat classless. All had a fondness for personal independence. All were intellectuals who lived as much by their intellectual accomplishments as by their political careers. None had the immediate or substantial middle-class financial interests which one might expect—nothing approaching, for example, the involvement of Laffitte in "haute bourgeoisie" banking or of the Peel family in industry. Lastly, it is well to remember that a good number of bona fide aristocrats—witness Earl Grey and de Broglie—also joined the *juste milieu* experiment on both sides of the Channel.

Although these comments by no means disprove the claim that class is an important influence in ideology, I do submit that a close analysis of the French and English *justes milieux* documents an argument rather different from Mannheim's statement of that claim. First, there does seem to exist such a thing as the middling mind—the mind which, regardless of class identity or political context, invariably craves the middle way. Second, the middling mind which is forever fascinated with *juste milieu* synthesis is also the very mind which is least able to succeed in that experiment. Third, that infirmity reflects, however, not so much the trap of class as it does the trap of political centrism. The problem is not simply that the person who is preoccupied with trimming is seldom

an original or exciting theorist. The more basic problem is
that the middling mind seems especially susceptible to either
a nightmare view of the present or a kind of reverie in the
present. It can seldom meet what Mannheim rightly suggests
as the crucial prerequisite for successful synthesis: "a peculiar
alertness to the historical reality of the present."[22] Caught in
the paradox of the center, the middling mind instead either
conjures up dangers which in fact do not exist, or loses itself
in the dream that the existing order already includes some
magic formula like the "general class" which will automatically adjust to all future needs. In either case, and however
often the middling mind may promise us a dynamic, eclectic
synthesis, its essential craving is "a general level, nowhere in
excess."

As a result, the fatal weakness of the middling mind is its
inability to cope for long with the problem of change in
human affairs. That is a weakness which it is understandably
reluctant to admit. In fact the *juste milieu* theorist usually
perpetrates something of a fraud by making a whipping boy
out of those who want to "go back" in history and recapture
the values of some golden age. According to perennial *juste
milieu* polemics, it is the conservatives who misunderstand
and cannot cope with change. The middling mind, in turn,
invariably makes a display of accepting as irrevocable the
change which has already occurred, including even revolution. More than that, it may seem to legitimize future change
by espousing some theory of progress. But sooner or later the
middling mind betrays itself. As Guizot confessed on one
occasion, "I have a horror of oblivion, of what passes away
quickly. Nothing pleases me so much as that which has the
air of durability and lasting memory."[23] For if the middling
mind tolerates past revolution, nothing seems more horrible
than the remote possibility of future revolution. If it envisions

---

[22] *Ibid.*, p. 154.   [23] *Embassy to St. James*, p. 127.

future progress, the smug assumption is that the values which will guide that progress are already determinate in the present.

But all this is fundamentally to misunderstand change. Change and progress, after all, involve human creativity. Although my conviction is that creativity is ultimately *indeterminate,* one need not accept that premise to follow my argument. It is sufficient simply to say that change is vastly more complex and mysterious than the middling mind assumes. It can never be immune to all excesses. It can never be limited to the explicit, observable values of the present. The essence of change, indeed, is that it will sooner or later significantly modify the values of the present with new ones, or with old ones recaptured from the past.

Thus the middling mind seldom satisfies the radical who wants to march bravely into the future or the conservative who promises to retrieve the golden past. And far more often than one might expect, both manage to survive the *juste milieu* effort to theorize them out of existence. Far more often than one might expect, both cope with change more effectively than the middling mind. In the case of the conservative, that is ironic indeed. It is true that history cannot be "turned back." Yet the militant look backwards—which one can find in a Burke or Disraeli as well as a Bonald or de Maistre—may well be what enables the conservative to go forward. The very attempt to recapture values of another age entails, after all, change. Despite all the conservative's emphasis on the mystery of history, man's fallibility, and the sanctity of prescription, the attempt also assumes that the future is not irrevocably determined by the present. Granted that the longing for the past can never quite be fulfilled, it has often involved a sufficiently hardheaded critique of the present to make the conservative come to terms with the reality of continuing change in human affairs.

That is precisely what the middling mind, caught in its unreal view of the present, cannot seem to do. And when the fleeting moment of the present is gone, the middling mind fails, leaving the field to those who look to man's two enduring horizons: the past and future.

MIDDLINGNESS
Juste Milieu Political Theory in
France and England, 1815–48

was composed, printed, and bound by
Kingsport Press, Inc., Kingsport, Tennessee.
The paper is Warren's Olde Style,
and the types are Granjon, Garamont, and
Garamond.
Design is by Edward Foss.

CALVIN T. RYAN LIBRARY
KEARNEY STATE COLLEGE
KEARNEY, NEBRASKA